CANCELLED

KU-615-295

SUNSHINE ON A PLATE

SIMPLE, VIBRANT COOKING TO WARM THE HEART

SHELINA PERMALLOO

EBURY PRESS

This book is dedicated to my dad. He has taught and continues to teach me so much, even though he is no longer here. He is my lifeline, the reason why I love to dream, always there and always with me. I love you Dad. This is the book you started for us but couldn't complete.

NORTH AYRSHIRE LIBRARIES	
06511740	
Bertrams	26/07/2013
641.596	£20.00
B	

NOTE ON INGREDIENTS

All eggs are medium and organic or free range unless otherwise stated. I use Billington's unrefined sugars.

Addresses for companies within the Random House Group can be found at www.randomhouse.co.uk

A CIP catalogue record for this book is available from the British Library

MIX
Paper from responsible sources
FSC® C004592

The Random House Group Limited supports the Forest Stewardship Council® (FSC®), the leading international forest-certification organisation. Our books carrying the FSC label are printed on FSC®-certified paper. FSC is the only forest-certification scheme supported by the leading environmental organisations, including Greenpeace. Our paper procurement policy can be found at www.randomhouse.co.uk/environment

To buy books by your favourite authors and register for offers visit www.randomhouse.co.uk

Text design and art direction by Smith & Gilmour
Photography by Martin Poole
Food stylists: Aya Nishimura & Richard Harris
Props stylist: Lydia Brun

Printed and bound by Firmengruppe APPL, aprinta druck, Wemding, Germany

ISBN 9780091950811

10 9 8 7 6 5 4 3 2 1

Published in 2013 by Ebury Press, an imprint of Ebury Publishing

A Random House Group Company

Text © Shelina Permalloo 2013
Photography © Ebury Press 2013

Shelina Permalloo has asserted her right to be identified as the author of this Work in accordance with the Copyright, Designs and Patents Act 1988

All rights reserved. No part of this publication may be reproduced, stored in a retrieval system, or transmitted in any form or by any means, electronic, mechanical, photocopying, recording or otherwise, without the prior permission of the copyright owner

The Random House Group Limited Reg. No. 954009

CONTENTS

Since winning *MasterChef* I have been inundated with requests from people asking me how to cook the food from the show, or telling me that they have been inspired to recreate some of my dishes. Every day on Twitter people ask me for recipes. I love the fact that there is so much interest, because the most important thing for me is that my food is accessible to all. The aim of this book is for the recipes to be as easy as possible in order to encourage you to have fun and to experiment with new flavours.

Every dish in this book has a memory attached to it, be it of my dad, mum, aunty, brother, sister or husband. After all, food is about sharing experiences with family and friends. Without them you wouldn't have the memories. Food has the ability to transport you to a time and place, and that is something I want people to feel when reading my book and preparing these dishes at home. I want the recipes to be shared among friends and family, and for this to be a book that is cooked from on a regular basis, a book you can get dirty, not one that sits in pristine condition on your kitchen shelf.

This book is an introduction to the homely cooking of Mauritius – food that is meant to be shared. I hope you enjoy the recipes as much as I do and have fun making them.

Mon Choisy – Friends, Family and Home

Mon Choisy was the name my parents gave to their first home in the UK. Although it was in Bitterne, Southampton, they named it after a beach on the West Coast of Mauritius. Dad used to go there with family and friends to eat salad, octopus, *gâteaux piments* (chilli cakes) and bread on the beach. Mon Choisy was the home I was born in so I have fond memories of my *Babam* (my grandmother on my dad's side) and *Amam* (my mum's mother) visiting, and remember lots of family members coming in and out of the house throughout my childhood.

My earliest memories of food are of sitting in the kitchen while my mum prepared our dinner. She'd give me a big wicker platter that was filled with pulses or rice and I would sit there sifting out the dirt and stones. Thank goodness for pre-cleaned and prepared rice now – it used to take me hours!

Mum always listens to music while cooking and when I think of the times I used to sit on a little stool in the kitchen being her sous chef, my head fills with memories of old Indian songs and traditional Mauritian Sega songs – classics like 'Bayaboo' and 'Li Tourner' – my mum humming away as she chopped garlic, ginger and onions, the clattering of the rolling pin and the sound of the pressure cooker steaming in the background. Dad would come in and try to dabble with Mum's cooking, but usually he would just pinch the best bits before it hit the table! That was one of the best things about staying in the kitchen with Mum; you got to nab the hot, fresh roti bread straight from the pan and dip it into the various stews and curries as she was cooking. I'm surprised anything made it to the table as it was all so delicious – but that's the other thing about Mum's cooking: there was always enough for seconds.

In 1994 my dad died. It was the biggest shock and left our family completely and utterly devastated. It was sudden and unexpected and to this day I still can't believe that he isn't with us. My mum had to learn very quickly how to take care of three children while working as a nurse every hour she could, just to make sure we had a roof over our heads.

Dad's biggest wish was that we should receive a good education and go to university, and Mum wanted to make sure that happened. When I was 13 years old we had to choose some form of work experience and I had spoken to Mum and Dad about exploring catering. They both wanted me to have more of a 'profession' and advised me to look into other career options. I only remembered their words when I was filming *MasterChef* and I asked

Mum why they had said no. She told me that she and Dad came to this country for a better life, and that education was the key to that. I listened to her and respected my dad's wishes, completing my degree before working in a variety of roles in project management.

Throughout my professional career I knew, deep down, that something was missing. I used to dream of having my own catering company where I could spend all day cooking, devising recipes and planning ways to have a party at home, just so that I could cook for my friends and family. It was a dream that would get me through my office days.

Mum is my cookery inspiration. Even when she was working a night shift, she would prepare dinner for us every evening and leave it on the stove for us. She made the most out of store-cupboard ingredients such as sardines, corned beef, dried fish and rice, and balanced every dish nutritionally – we never had a single dinner without vegetables. When Mum wasn't at work we would always sit around the table and eat dinner together. This was our way of connecting with each other and our cultural heritage. At the beginning of every meal we would say, 'Thanks, Mum, for our dinner', before ravenously tucking into the tasty food. Our house always smelled wonderful, and walking home from school I could smell Mum's cooking ten houses away. Even today Mum's house still smells the same and conjures up evocative memories.

It took me a while to work out that Mum would always leave things out when giving me her recipes. When I went off to university and tried to recreate her dishes I knew that it wouldn't taste *quite* like Mum's food. I think she did it so we would miss her food and come back home! I now understand why she did this, but growing up it was so frustrating. I remember speaking to her about her recipe for *gâteaux piments*. I tried for months and months but couldn't figure out why the recipe wasn't working. Eventually Mum decided to give me the 'complete' recipe, but only after I had been chosen for *MasterChef*! For all those years she didn't tell me that I had to soak the yellow split peas for a couple of hours, preferably overnight, to stop the cakes breaking up when they're deep-fried. It's funny because I know that if I have children I'll probably do exactly the same.

In 2007 I met my husband Andrea. He was born in Rome and moved over to London when he was 20. When I told him on our first date that I could make home-made gnocchi, it sealed the deal! In 2010 we got married in Mauritius, and 50 of our friends and family travelled from Rome and London to join us on the island to celebrate our marriage. Mum said she was going to keep it small but we still ended up with 300 guests... although, to be honest, that is a small wedding by Mauritian standards. It was the best holiday of my life and there's no more romantic place to get married.

The Taste of an Island

One of the most fantastic things about Mauritian food is the sheer diversity and complexity of the cultures it brings together. Mauritius has often been described as a melting pot and that's also true for the island's food, which is a brilliant mix of Creole, Indian, Chinese, European and African cuisines.

It's amazing to think that just under 400 years ago there was no population on Mauritius. The island was first discovered by Arab sailors in the 1600s, then the Portuguese who brought pigs and monkeys with them, followed by the Dutch who came with deer. The French arrived in 1715 and changed its name to 'Ile de France'. The French introduced fruit trees and spices, and ruled until the British took over in 1810, bringing with them British colonialism... To this day, Mauritians love their afternoon tea. Mauritian food has retained its strong French influences but over time these have been adapted with some exotic enhancements.

To understand Mauritian cooking you have to look at the different ethnic groups that make up the island. There are Creole-Mauritians, Franco-Mauritians, Indo-Mauritians and Sino-Mauritians. This incredible diversity of people and colonial history means that

Mauritian food is best described as true fusion. You can find dishes that suit all palates, from fiery hot curries, to slow-cooked, French-inspired stews to Chinese fried noodle dishes.

One of the staples on the island is rice, which was brought over by Indian and Chinese settlers. Rice is found in many guises and you'll discover that it's a key part of many Mauritian dishes. Noodle and vermicelli recipes are also plentiful. Mauritians use pulses in many different ways, and they're the reason a lot of the recipes in this book are gluten-free and vegetarian friendly. Mauritian desserts often contain pulses, grains and vegetables so these also offer great gluten-free and vegan options.

A lot of breads and cakes were introduced by the French, and are probably why Mauritians have an obsession with fresh bread, which is delivered to homes all over the island every morning. *Daube* is another classic Mauritian dish which was introduced by the French, originating in Provence in France. The Mauritian version includes dry sherry and potatoes.

There are a few key ingredients that crop up again and again in Mauritian cuisine: tomatoes, garlic, ginger and chilli. These are found in a number of dishes, from the European-inspired casseroles to curries and the famous *rougaille*, a spicy Creole tomato sauce. They are also used in a variety of pickles and chutneys or achards. Spices used on the island include saffron, cumin, cardamom and turmeric. Venison is found in stews and curries, and chicken is used in a lot of Chinese cooking. Seafood and fish are everywhere – as an island Mauritius has some of the best Indian Ocean fish on offer and, for me, eating fresh fish and seafood is the best part of any trip to Mauritius.

Anyone who has visited Mauritius will know that there is an abundance of fruit, including lychees, bananas, guavas, papayas, coconuts, pineapples and, of course, mangoes. Ripe fruit is eaten as it is, perhaps with a squeeze of lime juice, while unripe fruits are used in pickles and many savoury dishes such as Beef and Green Papaya Curry (see page 100). Bananas are eaten as the fruit we all love in the UK, in sweet tarts or fried to make the French-inspired banana beignets, but green or unripe bananas also feature heavily in pickles and curries. Guava is an incredibly evocative fruit for me, as I remember going guava picking when I first visited the island, walking through the lush vegetation collecting bagfuls of the fruit with my niece and nephew. Guava is used to make fresh juice as well as wonderfully fiery condiments and pickles. And finally, on to my fruit obsession…

Mangoes and Memories

It is safe to say that I have a serious and utterly distracting addiction to mangoes. I didn't realise quite how much I loved them until I was on *MasterChef*, when I ended up using them in so many dishes. Mango is another tropical fruit that is abundant on the island. Unripe mango is used in salads and for pickles, while fresh mango is eaten simply as it comes.

My mum told me how, when she was a little girl growing up in Mauritius, she used to walk through the fields and pick the mangoes from the floor. The fruits were so ripe she would just peel the skin off with her hands and walk along eating them, trying to catch the beautiful aromatic juice as it dripped down her hands.

When Mum moved to the UK at the age of nineteen, she missed many things about life on the island, but particularly the fresh fruit and vegetables. I now realise why I love mangoes so much. Growing up in Southampton, mangoes were not readily available so whenever Mum found them in ethnic shops and markets she would buy them as a treat for us all to share. Living in south London, I can buy them pretty much anywhere now, but the taste of fresh mango always reminds me just what a luxury they were while I was growing up. They remind me of the incredible journey my mum has made – perhaps that's why I still consider them such an indulgent treat.

Essential Ingredients, Spices and Techniques

Cardamom pods (green) These small green pods are used a lot in Mauritian cooking, in desserts and in savoury dishes as the spice has both savoury and sweet notes to it. Some recipes call for whole pods – often to infuse a dish with flavour, while others just use the seeds that are found inside the pods. Cardamom is best kept in pod form as once the seeds are removed they lose their flavour and fragrance very quickly.

Chilli In Mauritius chillies are eaten with pretty much everything. Mauritians use chilli in a variety of ways. A classic treat on the streets is to find fresh pineapple and mango, covered in sugar syrup, lemon juice and fresh chilli. Oddly enough, this sweet, salty, fruity and ferociously hot combination has a cooling effect in the tropical sun. The chilli I use most often is the bird's eye chilli. These small, thin, red or green chillies are found in Asian grocers and large supermarkets and are very hot. If you can't find bird's eye chillies you can use the larger chillies instead. It is sometimes difficult to gauge the heat of a chilli and it is so often down to personal taste so if you are not sure, it's a good idea to start with a smaller amount of chilli and then add more if you wish. I also like to leave the seeds in when I use chillies because I like the heat, but you can always seed them before using.

Cinnamon A sweet, smoky and fragrant spice used for both savoury and sweet dishes. It enhances the flavour of meat and is used frequently in desserts.

Coconut In Mauritius it's very common to see street vendors selling young green coconut water served straight from the coconut with a straw out of the top. This coconut water is deliciously refreshing and has a unique sweet and sour taste. The older brown coconut is finely grated, and is used to make a beautiful condiment called *satchini coco* (see page 168).

Coriander (fresh) This lovely fresh herb is used throughout southern Asia and Mauritius is no exception. It is used to flavour dishes and as a garnish. I tend to buy it fresh in bunches as you can just stick the coriander in a glass of water or store it in the fridge wrapped in a damp cloth and use as necessary. I hate waste so will often use the finely chopped stalks, which have just as much flavour, in my recipes.

Coriander seeds Coriander seeds have a completely different flavour to the fresh herb – their wonderful citrussy flavour works really well with fish and seafood. The seeds are warm and nutty and can be used whole or ground. You can buy ground coriander or grind the seeds yourself in a spice grinder or pestle and mortar.
To toast seeds Put a few tablespoons of seeds in a small heavy-based frying pan over a high heat – do not add any oil. Stir for a few minutes until the seeds start to turn darker and release their pungent aroma. Remove from the pan and allow to cool – they can be used as they are or ground in a pestle and mortar. Any unused toasted seeds can be kept for a few weeks in an airtight container.

Cumin seeds These have an unmistakable smell and are very nutty in flavour. They are used to season dishes and add subtle flavouring to rice and curries. Many recipes call for cumin seeds to be toasted – this releases their strong aroma.

Curry leaves These dark green leaves are used in curries and pickles and are usually fried in oil first to release their delicious lemony aroma. Use fresh curry leaves wherever possible as the dried ones do not have the same intensity of flavour.

Curry powder The key ingredients in a curry powder are generally ground coriander, cumin, turmeric and chilli but there are so many variations from country to country and region to region. For me, the smell of Mauritian curry powder is heady and aromatic and transports me back to eating curries surrounded by my family at big Mauritian parties. There are people in Mauritius who have been grinding and smoking curry powders for decades. I'm not in any way hoping to replicate their hard work, but I can show you how to make a simple curry powder at home that encapsulates the flavour of a real Mauritian curry powder.
To make Mauritian curry powder – the cheat's version Mix together 50g of mild madras curry powder, 20g of ground coriander, 20g of ground cumin and 10g of ground turmeric. Store in an airtight container, away from direct sunlight, for up to a month.
To make Mauritian curry powder from scratch To make a curry powder that most closely resembles the fragrant curry powder found on the island, first toast the spices. Put 40g of coriander seeds, 40g of cumin seeds, 20g of fennel seeds and 10g of fenugreek seeds in a smoking hot skillet or frying pan, and toast without oil for a couple of minutes, until the coriander seeds start to pop and the spices start to release their aromas. Allow to cool and then place the toasted spices in a spice grinder, along with half a small cinnamon stick, 10–15 dried curry leaves, 3 dried red chillies and 20g of ground turmeric. Grind until you have a fine powder. Place in an airtight container, away from direct sunlight, and use as soon as possible. It's best to make this in small batches so as not to lose the fragrance of the spices.

Fennel seeds These look quite similar to cumin seeds, but have a greenish colour and smell and taste of aniseed. They are a great accompaniment to fish, as well as pork and salads.

Fenugreek seeds These small hard seeds are bitter and tangy in flavour but work incredibly well with older meats such as mutton and goat. I use them to enhance the natural flavours of meat in long, slow-cooked curries.

Garam masala This is an Indian blend of spices, which includes black and white peppercorns, black and green cardamom pods, cinnamon, cloves and cumin seeds, although there are many regional variations. It is used alongside other spices and ingredients in curries, biriyanis and stews.

Ginger Fresh ginger is used throughout this book and is widely available in the UK. Most recipes call for a piece of fresh ginger that is then peeled and finely chopped or grated to a pulp. It is very often combined with garlic – if you go to the home of any Mauritian you will most likely find a jar in the fridge that contains garlic and ginger paste. *To make ginger and garlic paste* This paste is made by blending equal quantities of ginger and garlic. Peel the fresh root ginger and add to a food processor or blender along with the same quantity of peeled garlic cloves. Blitz until you have a smooth pulp, adding a little oil as you blend to get a smooth paste. Store in an airtight container and top with a little more oil. This will keep in the fridge for up to 10 days.

Mustard seeds These are used in pickles and curry powders, as well as in many curry dishes. Mustard seeds are often thrown into hot oil at the start of a dish where they pop and develop their characteristic aromatic, nutty flavour. You can find light and dark seeds – brown mustard seeds are the mostly widely used.

Paprika Wonderfully bright in colour, paprika varies from very hot to sweet, depending on the variety of capsicum it is made from. It is used to enhance a number of savoury dishes.

Parsley Flat-leaf parsley features in many dishes – more typically in those influenced by Mediterranean

cuisines. As with fresh coriander, you can buy this in bunches and keep it for several days in a glass of water or in the fridge, wrapped in a damp cloth.

Pulses Pulses are part of the everyday Mauritian diet. Yellow split peas are made into dahl soups, added to curries and soaked overnight to create delicious chilli cakes (*gâteaux piments*). Yellow and brown lentils are used in a range of soups, typically cooked with garlic, chilli, coriander and thyme. One of my favourite dishes growing up was lentils with rice and greens. Simple, frugal, vegan and incredibly tasty.

Saffron The Queen of Spices is the most expensive of all. Saffron comes from the dried stigma of the crocus and can only be picked by hand. The flavour is very difficult to describe – in my opinion it tastes both sweet and bitter. A little bit of saffron goes a long way towards colouring a dish and imparting its flavour.

Shallots Shallots are used to add texture, crunch and sweetness. Deep-fried shallots are used as a garnish in many Mauritian dishes. *To deep-fry shallots* Peel the shallots and slice thinly. Heat some vegetable oil in a deep pan – you need a depth of about 5cm – it is hot enough when a cube of bread dropped into the oil turns golden in 30 seconds. Alternatively heat the oil in a deep-fat fryer to 180°C. Carefully add the shallots and fry for a few minutes until golden and crisp. Remove from the oil, drain on kitchen paper and set aside to cool.

Star anise I think these are the prettiest spices – you could almost make a necklace using them! Reddish brown in colour, with a fantastic and unmistakable appearance, this spice has an aniseed flavour. It is used a lot in Chinese cooking and is one of the spices that make up five spice powder. Star anise is used frequently in desserts as well as in rich meat dishes.

Thyme This classic European herb is used a lot in French and Portuguese cooking. It's often found in stews and curries, and also in all my braised meat recipes.

Tomatoes Tomatoes – *pommes d'amour* – appear in many Mauritian dishes, whether Indian, Chinese, Creole or French in origin. They are the main ingredient in the Creole *rougaille* sauce and the French *daube*, and form the basis of a number of curries – as well as chutneys and salsas.

Turmeric When dried and ground turmeric produces a bright yellow powder. The beautiful vivid colour can stain hands and clothes so be careful. It's used extensively to create colour and also to impart an earthy and sharp flavouring. It is sometimes used as a cheaper alternative to saffron, where a yellow colour is required, but too much can make a dish taste like detergent, so use with care. Mauritians use both fresh and dried turmeric, particularly for the Indo-Mauritian inspired dishes, as well as in octopus, fish and vegetable pickles. However, fresh turmeric is not widely used in the UK so the recipes in this book call for ground turmeric.

Vanilla Sweet and perfumed vanilla is used almost everywhere in Mauritius, from flavoured rum to desserts and cakes. Vanilla is one of the most popular flavourings in the world. Although you can buy good-quality vanilla extract, using vanilla pods will give a much better flavour. Always keep the vanilla pods once you have removed the seeds – you can add it to a jar of caster sugar to make vanilla sugar or even to a bottle of rum! *To remove the seeds from a vanilla pod* Place the vanilla pod on a chopping board, and using the back of a knife, press firmly along the whole pod to flatten it. Slice the pod in half lengthways and then scrape out the seeds using the sharp edge of the knife.

GAJAKS
MAURITIAN APERITIVI

I am in love with *gajaks*. You may not be familiar with this quirky word. *Gajak* is a Mauritian Creole word that is the catch-all term for any food eaten before a main meal, or food that is snacked on during the day. It is similar to what the Italians call *aperitivi* or Spanish *tapas*: wonderful small plates of food served at a bar to nibble alongside your cold beer, glass of wine, or campari and soda. Anyone who knows me knows that I love to graze, particularly when I am at a restaurant: I much prefer to pick at lots of small dishes than sit down to a huge plateful. I find it a great way to eat as you get to sample lots of different foods without feeling too full.

Mauritian *gajaks* cover everything from small snacks eaten at home to delicious street food, but whatever form they take, the point is sharing. What could be better than enjoying a few drinks and some *gajaks* with friends and family? One of the most popular *gajaks* eaten in Mauritius is also my favourite: *Gâteaux Piments* (see page 22), which translates as 'chilli cakes'. These fiery, crunchy little balls made of yellow split peas and chilli are great with a bottle of cold Phoenix (the local beer). Another favourite is Spicy Aubergine Baja (see page 19), thin slices of aubergine in a chickpea flour batter, eaten with a hot chilli sauce. You can find *gajaks* across Mauritius in most small shops and bars, arranged in glass cabinets, along with a range of plastic dishes containing the condiments to go with them.

The ultimate street food in Mauritius is *Dal Puri* (see page 162). Street food vendors sell these wonderful flat breads everywhere, made with thin layers of ground yellow split peas to give an almost flaky consistency, filled with butter bean curry, chilli sauce and fresh coriander chutney. One of my fondest memories is of sitting on the beach with my sister when a street vendor drove past us on his moped with a container at the back. We quickly flagged him down and ordered our *dal puri* with all the extras. We sat back on the beach and watched the waves as we tucked into our favourite snack, not caring that all the juices were dripping on to our clothes. A perfect, memorable moment.

You can serve *gajaks* as you would a mezze, with a range of small plates to share, either to accompany some delicious cocktails and drinks (see pages 210–19) or as part of a relaxed dinner party or al fresco meal.

SOY SAUCE EGGS  SERVES 6-8

There is a flourishing Sino-Mauritian community in Mauritius and its influence can be seen in many of the island's staple dishes. This *gajak* has a definite Chinese flavour and is quite possibly one of the easiest snacks to make. In Mauritius you'll come across this dish all the time. The eggs work perfectly with cocktails or a light beer before a dinner party.

10 large eggs
500ml dark soy sauce
200ml oyster sauce

TO GARNISH
½ red onion, finely chopped
2 red chillies, seeded and finely
   chopped
3 tbsp freshly chopped coriander

1 Bring a large pan of water to the boil and hard-boil the eggs for about 8–10 minutes. Rinse under cold water and when cool enough to handle, remove the shells.

2 Put the soy sauce and oyster sauce in a bowl and add the peeled eggs. Leave to steep for at least 4–5 hours.

3 When you are ready to serve, slice the eggs into quarters and arrange on a large plate. Scatter with the red onion, chilli and coriander.

POTATO AND PEA SAMOSAS MAKES 20

These are a bit fiddly but making your own samosas at home is one of the most satisfying things you can do. Do as my Mum does: make them in bulk and freeze them so you always have them handy when guests come over.

1 tbsp vegetable oil, plus
  extra for deep-frying
1 shallot
1 tbsp Ginger and Garlic Paste
  (see page 11)
4 curry leaves
1 tbsp ground cumin
2 tbsp Mauritian curry powder
  (see page 10)

3 white potatoes, peeled and
  chopped into 2.5cm cubes
75g frozen peas
1 tbsp freshly chopped coriander
1 red bird's eye chilli, finely chopped
20 samosa wrappers or 1 packet
  of filo pastry (see Note)
salt and freshly ground black pepper

1 Heat the oil in a pan over a medium heat and fry the shallot until translucent. Add the ginger and garlic paste and then the curry leaves, ground cumin and Mauritian curry powder. Cook for about 1 minute, add the potatoes and cover immediately with a lid (the idea is to steam the potatoes a bit). Reduce the heat to low and cook for about 10 minutes.

2 After 10 minutes, check the mixture and if you find it too dry add a little bit of water to prevent it sticking to the pan. Remember: this isn't a curry, it should be thick enough to fill the samosas. When you notice the potato starting to break down, add the peas and cook for about 5 minutes – they just need to take on the spicy flavours from the pan. Add the fresh coriander and chopped chilli and season to taste.

3 To fill the samosas, take a samosa wrapper and place a tablespoon of the mixture at the top left corner of the rectangle. Fold the top right corner over the mixture to make a triangle. Fold this triangle over and keep going until you have a samosa. To bind the samosa together and to make sure the mixture doesn't come out, dab the corners with some water: this will act like a glue to stick the corners down. Be patient – once you have made a few you'll find a rhythm!

4 Heat enough oil for deep-frying in a large heavy-based pan until you start to see bubbles emerging from the bottom. Test the temperature with one samosa: if the samosa immediately bubbles and floats to the top, then the oil is hot enough. Alternatively use a deep-fat fryer.

Continued overleaf

5 Deep-fry the samosas in batches until golden. This normally takes about 4–5 minutes, but it will vary depending on the size of the wrappers and the amount of filling you put into them. You will know when they are cooked as they go a lovely golden brown colour and are much firmer in texture.

6 Remove with a slotted spoon and drain on kitchen paper. Serve immediately with Coriander and Mint Chutney (see page 166).

NOTE
Samosa wrappers can be found in Asian or Indian supermarkets and come in one size. Use filo pastry as an alternative but you will need to use two sheets at a time to keep the samosa intact. Cut the filo pastry into strips 10cm wide.

BREAD CROQUETTES
MAKES APPROXIMATELY 8 CROQUETTES

Ever wanted to do something a little different with your stale bread? Well, this is a brilliant way to give a spicy lift to day-old bread.

200g chickpea (gram) flour
1 tsp salt
1 tsp pepper
1 red chilli, finely chopped
1 garlic clove, finely chopped
1 tsp hot smoked paprika

4 pieces stale white bread, crusts removed and each slice cut into 2
vegetable oil for deep-frying
Satchini Pomme d'Amour (see page 166), to serve

1 Place all the ingredients except the bread and vegetable oil into a large bowl and mix together. Add about 160ml cold water to create a pancake-like batter, mixing well so the batter is smooth.

2 Heat enough oil for deep-frying in a large heavy-based pan to 180°C, or until a cube of day-old bread dropped in turns golden in 30 seconds. Alternatively use a deep-fat fryer. Dip the bread pieces into the batter and deep-fry until golden brown, about 1–2 minutes. Remove with a slotted spoon and drain on kitchen paper. Serve piping hot, with Satchini Pomme d'Amour.

SPICY AUBERGINE BAJA MAKES 10–12

I absolutely love aubergines. If I had my way I would use aubergines in every single dish. These *baja* are wonderfully light – even though they are deep-fried, the chickpea flour in the batter stops any oil from coming through so you are left with a deliciously steamed aubergine with a crunchy exterior. I use finger aubergines as I find them sweeter and less bitter than the bigger varieties usually found in supermarkets. The recipe works just as well with larger aubergines; you will just need to slice them slightly thinner so that they cook evenly.

200g chickpea (gram) flour
2 tsp salt
1 bunch fresh coriander, finely chopped
(leaves and stalks)
2 garlic cloves, finely chopped

2 red bird's eye chillies, finely chopped
160ml warm water
2 small finger aubergines (look in
Middle Eastern or Indian grocers)
vegetable oil for deep-frying

1 In a mixing bowl combine the chickpea flour, salt, coriander, garlic, chillies and warm water and stir together, adding more water if necessary, until you have a batter with the consistency of yoghurt.

2 Slice the aubergines into rounds. Heat enough oil for deep-frying in a large, heavy-based pan. Test if the oil is hot enough by dropping in a cube of day-old bread – it should turn golden in about 30 seconds. Alternatively, heat a deep-fat fryer to 180°C.

3 Dip the aubergines in the batter to coat them. Drop them carefully in the oil and deep-fry in batches until golden brown, about 4–5 minutes. Remove with a slotted spoon and drain on kitchen paper. Serve hot with a spicy chutney, such as Satchini Pomme d'Amour (see page 166), and Spicy Mauritian Coleslaw (see page 27). (Pictured on page 21.)

GATEAUX PIMENTS WITH CRAB

MAKES 15-20

These are one of my favourite *gajaks*. They don't usually include crab but I can't resist tweaking recipes and I find that the crab adds a depth of flavour and a lovely texture to these little chilli cakes. They get their crunch from the yellow split peas, which are soaked overnight but not pre-cooked. Enjoy these snacks with a cocktail, such as Mango Mojito with Spiced Cold Rum (see page 212).

100g yellow split peas, soaked in cold water overnight
2 bird's eye chillies, finely chopped
1 garlic clove, finely chopped

2 tbsp freshly chopped coriander
80g fresh white crabmeat
salt
vegetable oil for deep-frying

1 Drain the split peas, place in a food processor and pulse until you have a coarse paste. Transfer to a mixing bowl and add the chillies, garlic, coriander, crabmeat and salt to taste. Mix well and then roll into small balls, about the size of a walnut, using the palms of your hands.

2 Heat enough oil for deep-frying in a large, heavy-based pan. Test if the oil is hot enough by dropping in a cube of day-old bread – it should turn golden in about 30 seconds. Alternatively, heat a deep-fat fryer to 180°C. Deep-fry the cakes in batches for about 4 minutes until crisp and golden. Remove with a slotted spoon and drain on kitchen paper.

TOD MAN PLA MAKES 12-15

When I was on *MasterChef*, the final four contestants were flown to Thailand as part of the final challenge. I was completely overwhelmed as I had wanted to go there for years. When we first arrived I went straight out on to the streets to see what was happening. I was amazed by the variety of street food available and the wonderful produce in the markets. I completely fell in love with Thailand and have been inspired to use its cooking techniques and flavour combinations. This fish cake recipe is just one recipe based on what I learned in the street markets of Chiang Mai. I've used whole crushed coriander seeds; they have a wonderful citrussy undertone that is nothing like the fresh herb but actually works very well with fish and shellfish.

300g skinless red sea bream fillets or any firm white fish such as snapper or red mullet
2 tsp ground coriander
1 tsp coriander seeds, crushed
1 tbsp turmeric
2.5cm piece of fresh root ginger, peeled and grated
3 garlic cloves, finely chopped
1 red chilli, finely chopped
salt and freshly ground black pepper
vegetable oil for frying

1 Put all the ingredients, except the oil, into a food processor and blitz until you have a smooth paste.

2 Heat a generous amount of oil in a deep frying pan over a medium heat – you want about 5cm of oil in the pan. Take a tablespoon of the fish mixture and drop it carefully into the oil. Cook the fish cakes in batches for about 4–5 minutes, turning them occasionally to get an even colour. Serve immediately with some ginger and chilli paste (see Haloumi with Ginger and Chilli Paste, page 44).

CHICKEN WITH RED ONIONS

SERVES 4-6

This is delicious to share as part of a *gajak*, but equally you could have it as a main meal and serve it next to a simple salad. It's perfect for a summer evening. In this recipe I have left the chicken thighs whole as I find that the wonderful brown meat stays moist when it is cooked on the bone. If you prefer, you can use boneless thighs.

400g chicken thighs, skinned
3 tbsp vegetable oil
2 tbsp dark soy sauce
3 spring onions, finely chopped
1 red onion, thinly sliced
2 large red chillies, roughly chopped
salt and freshly ground black pepper

TO GARNISH
1 red chilli, sliced
2 shallots, deep-fried (see page 11)

1 Use a heavy knife to make shallow cuts in the chicken thighs, making sure they retain their shape. Heat the oil in a large wok and add the thighs. Brown on all sides – this takes around 5–7 minutes.

2 Once they are nice and brown, add the soy sauce, spring onions and salt and pepper and cook for around 10 minutes with the lid on – you are looking for quite a sticky consistency. Add the sliced red onion along with the chillies and cook for a further 5 minutes. Remove from the heat and garnish with chilli and deep-fried shallots.

SPICY MAURITIAN COLESLAW SERVES 6-8

Traditionally the vegetables and chillies in this dish are 'julienned'
(cut into very fine strips of equal size). Leaving the chillies in long strips
means that when you think are eating a green bean you may actually
be eating a fiery chilli! You can chop the chilli finely but I prefer leaving
them in strips for that little frisson of danger.

5 tbsp vegetable oil
3 tbsp mustard seeds
2 garlic cloves, finely chopped
5–10 green chillies (depending on how
    hot you like it!), halved lengthways
2 tsp ground turmeric

1 small shallot, finely chopped
100g white cabbage, shredded
100g carrots, peeled and julienned
100g green beans, julienned (see above)
1 tbsp salt
2 tbsp white wine vinegar

1 Heat the oil in a large pan over a medium heat and add the mustard
seeds. When they start to 'pop' in the pan, add the garlic, chillies, turmeric
and about 3 tablespoons of water. Cook, stirring, until you have a paste –
this should take about 3 minutes.

2 Add the shallot and cook for 1–2 minutes; then add the cabbage, carrots,
beans and salt. Cook for about 2–3 minutes until well combined and then
remove from heat (you don't want the vegetables to lose their crunch). Stir
in the white wine vinegar and check the seasoning – you may need to add
more salt.

3 Leave to cool before serving with bread or pan-fried fish. The coleslaw
will keep for up to 7 days in an airtight container in the fridge.

CHICKEN AND PORK STEAMED DUMPLINGS

MAKES 20

These are very much like dim sum; another Mauritian dish with Chinese origins. Usually they would be eaten before *Min Frire* (see page 154) or *Pork Bol Renversé* (see page 146). These may sound complex but if you buy ready-made dumpling wrappers, it's really a very simple dish, which I guarantee you will absolutely love.

20 dumpling wrappers (look in specialist Asian supermarkets)
100g minced pork
100g minced chicken
1 tsp palm sugar
1 tbsp light soy sauce
2 small banana shallots, finely diced
2 garlic cloves, very finely chopped
2.5cm piece of fresh root ginger, peeled and very finely chopped

1 tsp sesame oil
1 tsp rice wine vinegar
1 tsp white pepper
vegetable oil, for brushing

TO GARNISH
3 spring onions, roughly chopped
2 large red chillies, roughly chopped

1 Dumpling wrappers are usually sold frozen so set them aside to defrost thoroughly. Meanwhile, place all the other ingredients except the vegetable oil, into a bowl and mix well with your hands to create a smooth paste.

2 Take a dumpling wrapper and place in front of you. Put a teaspoon of the mixture into the centre of the wrapper, moisten all four sides of the wrapper and then bring together with your hand to create a parcel. Moisten the top and press together. Repeat this process with all the other wrappers.

3 Place a bamboo steamer over a large wok of water covering about 12cm of the base. Brush the base of the steaming basket with a little oil – this is to stop the dumplings sticking. Place the dumplings inside and steam for around 7–8 minutes. Once cooked, remove from the steamer, scatter with the chopped spring onion and chilli and serve.

CHO-CHO AND PRAWN BALLS

MAKES 15-20

Cho-cho, also known as pear squash, chouchoute or choko, is a member of
the squash family and can be used both raw and cooked. You can normally
find cho-cho in specialist Asian supermarkets, they look like old knobbly
pears that are bright green in colour. If you can't get hold of cho-cho you
can use marrow, which has a similar taste and texture when cooked.

100g peeled brown shrimps
400g cho-cho, peeled, cored and grated
60g tapioca flour
1 tbsp light soy sauce

2 banana shallots, finely chopped
1 garlic clove, grated
Satchini Pomme d'Amour
  (see page 166), to serve

1 Chop the shrimps thoroughly to create a fine shrimp mince and place
in a large bowl. Add all the other ingredients and mix well.

2 Line a bamboo steamer with some parchment paper and set over a pan
of simmering water. Roll the mixture into small balls, about the size of
an apricot, and place into the steamer. Steam for about 20 minutes until
cooked all the way through – they will be translucent when done. Serve
immediately with the Satchini Pomme d'Amour.

TAMARIND RED BREAM

MAKES 12–15 PIECES

Tamarind, with its sweet-and-sour flavour, works really well with fish. You may need to make double of this as it disappears quickly.

400g red bream fillet, cut into
   5cm cubes
vegetable oil for deep-frying
Thai Dipping Sauce (see page 171),
   to serve

FOR THE MARINADE
50g tamarind pulp, soaked in
   200ml warm water for 4 hours
1 tbsp light brown muscovado sugar
1 garlic clove, grated
1 tbsp finely chopped coriander stalk
2.5cm piece of fresh root ginger,
   peeled and grated
1 tbsp light soy sauce
juice of 1 lime
2 tbsp cornflour

1 Start by preparing the marinade. Drain the tamarind pulp by squashing the mixture through a sieve. You will be left with a thick pulp. Put this pulp into a large mixing bowl with all the other marinade ingredients and mix well.

2 Add the cubes of red bream and stir gently so that all the pieces are covered. Chill in the fridge for about 20 minutes.

3 Heat enough vegetable oil for deep-frying in a large heavy-based pan. Test if the oil is hot enough by dropping in a cube of day-old bread – it should turn golden in about 30 seconds. Alternatively, if you have a deep-fat fryer, set the temperature to about 180°C. Place the cubed fish into the oil and fry for approximately 3 minutes, turning occasionally, until golden brown on all sides.

4 Serve immediately with the Thai Dipping Sauce.

CHILLI STUFFED WITH SARDINE MAKES 15

I was brought up eating quite a bit of tinned fish, mainly because fresh fish was very expensive when I was a child. Because of this I'm partial to tinned sardines and pilchards. I know it sounds a bit retro but you get an intense flavour from tinned sardines, which works perfectly with the piquancy of the chilli. You could also make a vegetarian version of this dish using a mix of beans instead of the sardines.

15 large long green chillies, such as Californian green chillies
2 x 120g tins sardines in sunflower oil, drained

1 banana shallot, finely chopped
1 red bird's eye chilli, finely chopped
1 spring onion, finely chopped
salt and freshly ground black pepper

1 Preheat the oven to 200°C/gas 6.

2 Carefully slit the chillies along one side and remove the seeds with a knife.

3 Place the drained sardines in a bowl and add the remaining ingredients. Mix together until you have a coarse paste. Use this mixture to stuff the inside of the chillies, being careful not to split the chillies as you want them to keep their shape.

4 Put the chillies on a roasting tray and place in the oven for around 12 minutes. Serve immediately.

VEGETARIAN VARIATION
Replace the sardines with 50g cooked kidney beans and 50g cooked borlotti beans. Mash the beans lightly before mixing with the other ingredients. Continue as above.

SPICY CRAB COURGETTE FLOWERS MAKES 10

Courgette flowers are absolutely gorgeous and are generally in season from early summer for around two months. You can still get hold of them at other times of the year but they will have been flown in from overseas.

100g fresh white crabmeat
1 red chilli, finely chopped
1 tsp white wine vinegar
1 tsp freshly chopped flat-leaf parsley

10 baby courgettes with flowers
1 tbsp olive oil
salt and freshly ground black pepper

1 Mix together the crabmeat, chilli, white wine vinegar, parsley and seasoning and carefully fill the courgette flowers with the mixture. Twist the top of each flower to make sure that no filling comes out when cooking. Be careful not to overfill them – even though it is incredibly tempting!

2 Once you have stuffed all the flowers, heat the oil in a frying pan over a medium heat and add the courgettes. Cook on all sides for around 6–7 minutes, you will know when they are cooked as the flowers take on a dark orange colour and will be lightly browned on all sides. Don't overcook these as you want the courgette still to have some bite to it. Serve immediately.

SNAPPER RISSOLES MAKES 8

I came up with the idea for these when I had some leftover pieces of snapper. Traditionally rissoles are wrapped in pastry but here I've used chickpea (gram) flour instead of plain flour as it keeps the rissoles light and airy.

150g snapper fillet, finely chopped
2 small shallots, finely chopped
2 garlic cloves, grated
1 tbsp freshly chopped coriander stalks
1 tsp crushed coriander seeds
½ beaten egg

1 tsp hot paprika
50g chickpea (gram) flour
2 tbsp vegetable oil
salt and freshly ground black pepper
Spicy Remoulade (see page 171),
  to serve

1 Place all of the ingredients except the chickpea flour, oil and seasoning into a food processor and blitz until completely combined. Divide the mixture into eight and roll into balls.

2 Mix the chickpea flour with some salt and pepper in a shallow dish and roll each rissole in the seasoned flour.

3 Heat the oil in a pan over a medium heat and shallow-fry the rissoles for around 10 minutes, turning occasionally, until they are cooked through and golden brown on all sides.

4 Serve immediately with the Spicy Remoulade.

CHICKEN LIVERS WITH WILD GARLIC LEAVES SERVES 6-8

Some people are completely put off by liver but this is most likely because it is so often overcooked. In this recipe the liver should still be soft. If you can't get hold of wild garlic leaves, you can use garlic chives instead.

250g chicken livers
1 tbsp vegetable oil
1 large Spanish onion
2 spring onions, finely chopped
2 garlic cloves, finely chopped

2 dried chillies
10–15 wild garlic leaves,
    roughly torn
salt and freshly ground black pepper
crusty white baguette, to serve

1 Slice the chicken livers in half and remove the white core and any membrane. Set aside.

2 Heat the oil in a large frying pan over a medium heat and add half the onion. Fry for about 2 minutes until slightly softened, then add the spring onions, garlic, pepper and dried chillies and cook for a further 2 minutes.

3 Add the livers and cook for around 2 minutes, then add 3 tablespoons of water and the remaining onion and cook for another few minutes. Remove from the heat, taste and adjust the seasoning and scatter over the wild garlic leaves. Serve immediately with a crusty white baguette.

GARLIC AND CORIANDER KING PRAWNS MAKES 6 SKEWERS

This is a great dish to make for a party as it's so simple.

3 garlic cloves, grated
juice and zest of 1 lime
1 tsp chilli powder
1 tsp coriander seeds,
  crushed

pinch of salt
18 large raw king prawns, shelled
  and deveined but tails left on
1 tbsp freshly chopped coriander,
  to serve

1 If you are using wooden skewers soak them in cold water for 30 minutes before using – this is to stop them getting charred during cooking.

2 Mix together all the ingredients except the prawns and fresh coriander in a large mixing bowl. Add the prawns and stir through the mixture until they are completely covered. Thread three prawns on to each skewer, making sure you push the skewer through the back of the prawn.

3 When all the prawns have been skewered, place on a preheated griddle or barbecue and cook for about 2 minutes on each side until the prawns have cooked all the way through and turned from grey to pink. Scatter over the chopped coriander and serve. (Pictured on page 41.)

SPICY BEEF PATTIES

MAKES 12–15 PATTIES

These are great to share before a main meal, however they work equally well as larger patties to fill a burger bun and are great to barbecue as well.

1 tbsp sunflower oil, plus extra
   for frying
2 tbsp chopped spring onion
2 garlic cloves, grated
1 tsp pink peppercorns, crushed
1 tsp ground turmeric
400g lean minced beef

2 tbsp freshly chopped coriander
1 tbsp freshly chopped mint
½ red Scotch Bonnet, seeded
   and finely chopped
1 egg, beaten
1 tsp fish sauce
1 tsp light soy sauce

1 Heat the oil in a large frying pan and add the spring onion, garlic, peppercorns and turmeric and cook for a few minutes until soft. Allow to cool slightly and then tip into a large mixing bowl. Add the minced beef to the bowl with all the remaining ingredients and mix well to combine. Shape the mixture into 12–15 patties, using your hands.

2 Heat some more oil in the same pan that you cooked the spring onions in and fry the patties until they are cooked through, about 3–4 minutes on each side. Drain on kitchen paper and serve immediately.

HALOUMI WITH GINGER AND CHILLI PASTE SERVES 3-4

This dish uses Thai 'scud' chillies – so called because of the way they sneak up on you and blast you with heat. Any other hot chilli, such as bird's eye, will work here.

250g haloumi
vegetable oil for frying
6 large red chillies, seeded and finely chopped
1 tbsp freshly chopped coriander
3 shallots, deep-fried (see page 11)

FOR THE GINGER AND CHILLI PASTE
5 dried red chillies
2 Thai 'scud' chillies
4 tsp Ginger and Garlic Paste (see page 11)
3 tbsp vegetable oil
2 tbsp unrefined light muscovado sugar
salt

1 To make the paste, place the dried chillies in a bowl of boiling water and leave for about 30 minutes. Remove the chillies from the water and retain some of the soaking water to use to make the paste. Place the chillies (soaked and fresh), ginger and garlic paste, oil, sugar and salt in a food processor or blender with a little of the reserved chilli soaking liquid and blitz until you have a thick paste.

2 Place the chilli paste in a pan and cook over a medium heat for about 10 minutes. Add some water if the mixture seems too thick, although it should resemble jam when cooked. Transfer to a small serving bowl.

3 Cut the haloumi lengthways into 2cm slices. Heat a little oil in a frying pan and cook the haloumi for a few minutes on each side until golden brown. Scatter over the chopped chillies, fresh coriander and deep-fried shallots and serve with the ginger and chilli paste.

NOTE
You can make the ginger and chilli paste in advance and store it in the fridge in a sterilised jar with a tight-fitting lid for up to 5 days.

MOOLKOO

I don't know whether 'moolkoo' is the right spelling but this is how we pronounce it in our house! That is what I love about Creole, it's a constantly evolving language. These are the most moreish snacks to have with a pre-dinner drink; a bit like Bombay mix. Once you have one, it's hard to stop. You can make a big batch of these and keep them in an airtight container for 2–3 weeks, although I can't promise they will be around for long.

350g rice flour
100g chickpea (gram) flour
1 tbsp ground cumin
1 tbsp cumin seeds, toasted
  (see page 10)
1 tsp chilli powder

1 tsp salt
75g unsalted butter, softened
  to room temperature
250–350ml water, or enough
  to create a soft paste
vegetable oil for deep-frying

1 Place all the dry ingredients in a large bowl and mix until well combined. Add the butter and water, a little at a time, and use your hands to make a soft dough. Add a little more water if the dough is too stiff – you need it to be soft enough to pipe through a piping bag.

2 Lightly oil the inside of a piping bag – this is to stop the dough from sticking. Fit the piping bag with a large open star nozzle.

3 Heat enough vegetable oil for deep-frying in a large heavy-based pan or wok. Test if the oil is hot enough by dropping in a cube of day-old bread – it should turn golden in about 30 seconds. Alternatively, if you have a deep-fat fryer, set the temperature to 180°C.

4 Place the dough inside the piping bag and pipe directly into the pan or fryer. Try and create overlapping circles and use scissors to cut off the dough at the nozzle. The moolkoo will take about 7 minutes to cook – they need to be nicely brown all over and should snap when cooked properly. Remove from the oil and drain on kitchen paper. Keep going, cooking in batches, until the dough is all used up. (Pictured on page 47.)

TREASURES FROM THE SEA
FISH

I absolutely adore fish and seafood; the possibilities for cooking and enjoying them are endless. From a fresh oyster shucked in its shell, to a tantalising lobster curry, to a simple baked sea bass, the versatility of fish and seafood never ceases to amaze me.

I think a lot of people are nervous about cooking fish, mainly because of the fear of either under- or overcooking it. I hope these recipes help you to feel more confident about our creatures of the sea. When my parents first came to the UK, the variety of fish and seafood available was obviously very different to that found back in Mauritius, with its incredible plethora. Fresh fish was often hard to get hold of and sometimes expensive, so Mum would improvise with frozen or tinned fish in order to reproduce the flavours that we knew and loved. For this reason I still have a real fondness for tinned fish, even though I have wonderful fresh fish available on my doorstep now.

In this chapter I have included classic Mauritian dishes, as well as some new combinations, such as fish and seafood with fruit. I hope you enjoy these recipes as much as I do.

OCTOPUS SALAD SERVES 6-8

Octopus is pretty much my all-time favourite seafood. When I was on *MasterChef*, one of my fellow contestants asked me what I would have for my last supper, and I said it had to be octopus! This dish is summery and light and is perfect to bring along to a barbecue or even served as part of antipasti.

Here's a top tip: always freeze your octopus before using it (check it has not already been frozen when you buy it). Freezing breaks down the mollusc structure, essential if you want soft, tender octopus. Other techniques include bashing the octopus over rocks for an hour, or adding a cork to the water when cooking... none of which I've found to be as good as freezing.

500g frozen octopus, completely thawed, head and tentacles removed and chopped into 2.5cm pieces
2 carrots, peeled and cut into very fine strips
2 celery sticks, sliced into crescents
2 banana shallots, finely chopped
3 tbsp freshly chopped flat-leaf parsley
3 tbsp freshly chopped coriander
2 tbsp freshly chopped garlic chives
2–3 tbsp extra-virgin olive oil
juice of 2 limes
salt and freshly ground black pepper
fresh bread, to serve

1 Bring a large pan of salted water to the boil, and add the octopus tentacles. Simmer for 1 hour.

2 Meanwhile mix together all the other ingredients in a large serving dish or bowl. Drain the octopus thoroughly and add to the serving dish while still warm. Mix together and leave to stand for at least 1 hour before eating as this will enable all the flavours to meld together.

3 Serve with fresh bread.

RED MULLET AND FENNEL

SERVES 4

1 banana shallot, finely sliced
4 large fennel bulbs, finely sliced
2 tbsp freshly chopped coriander
1 large red chilli, seeded and
   finely sliced
juice of 2 limes
1 tbsp fish sauce

1 tsp dark brown sugar
2 tbsp mustard oil
4 tbsp coriander seeds
250g red mullet fillets
2 tbsp olive oil
salt and freshly ground black pepper
fresh bread, to serve

1 Place the shallot, fennel, chopped coriander and chilli in a large bowl and add the lime juice. Whisk together the fish sauce, sugar, mustard oil and seasoning and pour over the salad. Toss to combine.

2 Use a pestle and mortar to crush the coriander seeds and then rub these over the red mullet fillets. Season with salt and pepper.

3 Heat the olive oil in a large frying pan and fry the fillets for 3 minutes on each side, until golden brown and cooked through. Break the fillets up and add to the salad. Serve with some fresh bread.

RED SNAPPER COCONUT CURRY

SERVES 4

5 tbsp vegetable oil
600g red snapper fillets
2 banana shallots, finely diced
3 garlic cloves, finely chopped
3cm piece of fresh root ginger,
  peeled and finely chopped
1 red bird's eye chilli, finely chopped
10 curry leaves
3 tbsp Mauritian curry powder
  (see page 10)

3–4 fresh vine tomatoes,
  roughly chopped
1 tsp tomato purée
1 x 200g block creamed coconut
600ml hot fish stock
3 tbsp freshly chopped coriander
salt and freshly ground black pepper
steamed basmati rice (see page 144),
  to serve
Mango Kutcha (see page 174), to serve

1 Heat the oil in a large pan over a high heat. When the oil starts smoking, add the fish, skin-side down, and stand back! Fry for 2 minutes on each side, remove from the heat and set aside.

2 Drain about half the oil from the pan and reduce the heat to medium. Add the shallots and fry until translucent, about 3 minutes, then add the garlic, ginger and chilli and cook for a further 2 minutes. Add the curry leaves and Mauritian curry powder and cook for 30 seconds before adding the chopped tomatoes and tomato purée. Cook down for 2–3 minutes until softened and the pan becomes dry.

3 Add the creamed coconut to the hot fish stock and stir until dissolved; add to the pan and cook for 15 minutes until the sauce has thickened. Taste and adjust the seasoning before adding the cooked fish fillets to the pan. Heat through for a few minutes, sprinkle over the coriander and serve with steamed basmati rice and Mango Kutcha. (Pictured on page 55.)

La Case La Paille
SNACK
Poisson
Grille
Menu Variés
TAKE AWAY

MAURITIAN CRAB BOUILLABAISSE

SERVES 6

This is a very typical starter in Mauritius, a chilli-hot soup packed with soft and succulent sweet crabmeat. It's absolutely delicious, and once you have finished the spicy, fragrant soup you can pick or suck the crabmeat from the shells.

3–4 tbsp vegetable oil
2 banana shallots, finely chopped
3 garlic cloves, finely chopped
3–5 red chillies, finely chopped (add
  more or less depending on your taste)
2 tbsp freshly chopped coriander stalks
1 tsp fresh thyme leaves

2 freshly cooked crabs (any kind),
  broken into pieces with claws
  cracked (see Note)
2 litres fish stock
200g good-quality tomato passata
salt and freshly ground black pepper

1 In a large casserole heat the vegetable oil over a medium to high heat. Add the shallots and cook until translucent, followed by the garlic, chillies, coriander stalks and thyme. Cook for a further 2 minutes to release the aroma from the thyme.

2 Add the crab pieces and cook for 5 minutes, then add the stock, passata and seasoning and cook for another 10 minutes. Cracking the claws will allow the soup to become infused with the crab flavour.

3 Remove the crab pieces from the pan and then reduce the bouillon for about 20–25 minutes over a medium heat – this stops the crab from overcooking. Return the crab to the bouillon just before serving.

NOTE
Ask your fishmonger to chop the crabs into pieces for you if you are squeamish about this bit.

LA DAUBE ORITE SERVES 6-8

This is a Mauritian octopus stew and is French in origin, which is evident in the use of thyme and tomatoes. It's an adaptation of the traditional *daube de boeuf* (beef stew) using seafood. The slow cooking intensifies the flavour of the octopus and ensures it is meltingly tender.

1kg frozen octopus
4 tbsp vegetable oil
1 large shallot, thinly sliced
3 garlic cloves, finely chopped
2 small red chillies, finely chopped
6 sprigs of thyme, leaves picked

½ x 400g tin whole plum tomatoes
800ml hot water
1 tbsp freshly chopped coriander
1 tbsp chopped spring onions
salt and freshly ground black pepper

1 Allow the octopus to thaw completely, wash thoroughly then cut into 5cm pieces.

2 Heat the oil in a large heavy-based pan over a medium heat. Add the shallot, garlic, chillies, thyme and black pepper and cook for about 3 minutes. Add the octopus and tomatoes and cook, stirring, for 15 minutes. Add the water, reduce the heat and simmer for 45–55 minutes.

3 Check the octopus is lovely and soft, if not, continue cooking until it softens. Every mollusc is different so cooking times may vary. Taste and adjust the seasoning.

4 To finish the stew, sprinkle over the coriander and spring onions and serve with a salad or some steamed basmati rice (see page 144).

ROUGAILLE POISSON SALE SERVES 4

Salted fish (*poisson salé*) is widely used in Mauritian cooking, along with dried shrimps. It has a really deep, salty flavour and a firm texture which holds up well during cooking. You'll need to soak the fish overnight in water, then rinse the fish three times in running water, allowing the fish to soak in water for 15 minutes in between each rinse. This is vital otherwise you will end up tasting salt and not fish.

4 tbsp vegetable oil
400g salted cod, soaked overnight
   in water, drained, rinsed three
   times and flaked into pieces
1 shallot, finely chopped
3 garlic cloves, finely chopped

1 bird's eye chilli, finely chopped
4 sprigs of thyme
1 x 400g tin plum tomatoes
2 tsp snipped chives
salt and freshly ground black pepper

1 Heat half the oil in a frying pan over a medium heat and add the salted cod. Fry for a few minutes until it starts to turn golden and then remove from the heat.

2 In a separate frying pan, heat the remaining oil and sauté the shallot, garlic, chilli and thyme for about 3 minutes. Add the plum tomatoes, along with their juice, and cook for 15 minutes, until the sauce starts to thicken. Reduce the heat and continue to cook for another 10 minutes, stirring to prevent the sauce from sticking.

3 Add the salt cod and stir gently to warm through. Taste and adjust the seasoning – you may not need to add any salt because of the saltiness of the cod. Sprinkle with the chives and serve.

VINDAYE POISSON SERVES 4-6

Vindaye fish is typical in Mauritius and can be made with any fish or even octopus. It is pretty much a pickle, similar to soused fish, using turmeric, mustard seeds and chilli. You can eat this on the same day, but the longer you leave it, the more potent the flavour becomes. I love eating it the day after with some warm crusty bread, like a baguette; it's absolutely delicious.

In Mauritius, you see vans parked up on the beach that are selling *vindaye poisson* or *vindaye orite* in large crusty baps. Whenever my brother is in Mauritius, you will find him on the beach with a *vindaye poisson* sandwich in one hand and a bottle of Phoenix (the local beer and the perfect companion) in the other. Just imagine sitting on the beach, watching the sunset, eating a wonderfully spiced fish sandwich with a cold beer in your hand. That's the food I dream about.

3 tbsp vegetable oil, plus extra
   for drizzling
600g firm skinless fish fillets such as
   tuna, snapper, grouper or mahi mahi,
   cut into 5cm pieces
2 large Spanish onions, sliced
6 garlic cloves, peeled but left whole
2 red chillies, thinly sliced

2.5cm piece of fresh root ginger,
   peeled and thinly sliced
2 tsp black mustard seeds
2 tsp ground turmeric
3–4 bay leaves
1 tsp sugar
½ tsp salt
200ml white wine vinegar

1 Heat the oil in a skillet or large frying pan and add the fish fillets. Cook for about 1 minute on each side. The fish should be underdone, as it needs to soak up the pickling liquor. Remove the fish from the pan and place in a plastic, lidded container.

2 Add the onions to the same pan the fish was fried in and cook for a few minutes over a medium heat. Add all the remaining ingredients, except the vinegar, and cook for 3 minutes.

3 Tip the contents of the pan over the cooked fish and then pour over the vinegar along with a good drizzle of oil. Allow to cool, then cover and chill in the fridge for several hours, preferably overnight.

BOULETTE POISSON SOUP SERVES 4–5

This Sino-Mauritian dish, with its fragrant aromas of coriander and chilli and steamed fish balls (*boulettes*), is surprisingly easy to make. I love eating it when I'm feeling slightly under the weather or when it's cold and wet outside! If you like, you can just make the fish balls and serve them with a spicy chutney such as *Satchini Pomme d'Amour* (see page 166).

FOR THE BOULETTES
400g pollock fillet
4 whole spring onions, trimmed
15ml rice wine vinegar
25ml light soy sauce
1 egg white
1 garlic clove
pinch of dried chilli flakes

FOR THE BROTH
1.2 litres fish stock
100g cooked brown shrimps, peeled
2 spring onions, finely chopped
1 tbsp freshly chopped coriander

1 Place all the ingredients for the boulettes into a food processor and blitz until you have a smooth paste. Rub a little oil on to the palms of your hands and start rolling the mixture into small balls – about the size of a lychee. Place on a non-stick tray.

2 In a large pan, bring the fish stock to a simmer and place the fish balls directly into the water. Cook for 10 minutes until the balls are firm to the touch and cooked all the way through.

3 Add the brown shrimps, chopped spring onion and coriander and serve.

SPICY SOFT-SHELL CRAB SERVES 4

I made this dish on *MasterChef* just after I'd worked with a 3-star Michelin Chef in Bruges. What I learned from that experience is that to be an excellent chef you have to love everything you cook. When I cooked this on the show it made John Torode very emotional and resulted in him telling me, 'you've come home'. This was a pivotal moment for me, as I realised that really excellent food can move people almost to tears. So John, this recipe is for you.

Soft-shell crabs come frozen in the UK so defrost thoroughly before cooking and dry completely with kitchen paper.

1 tbsp garam masala
1 tbsp ground turmeric
1 tsp ground coriander
1 tsp ground cumin
2 tsp dried mango powder
1 tbsp chilli powder
100g chickpea (gram) flour
100g rice flour

8 garlic cloves, peeled and crushed
  to a paste
5cm piece of fresh root ginger,
  peeled and grated
pinch of salt
3 tbsp finely chopped fresh coriander
4 soft-shell crabs
vegetable oil for deep-frying

1 Place all the dried spices, the chickpea flour and the rice flour in a large bowl and stir to combine. Gradually add cold water, about 200–250ml, and stir until you have a thick, smooth batter. Stir in the garlic, ginger, salt and chopped coriander until well combined. Drop the soft-shell crabs into the batter and leave for 10 minutes.

2 Heat enough vegetable oil for deep-frying in a large, heavy-based pan. Test if the oil is hot enough by dropping in a cube of day-old bread – it should turn golden in about 30 seconds. Alternatively, if you have a deep-fat fryer, set the temperature to 180°C.

3 Remove the crabs from the batter and shake off any excess. Gently lower the soft-shell crabs into the hot oil and fry for 2–4 minutes, until the shells of the crabs turn red. You will probably need to cook these in batches.

4 Remove the crabs from the pan using a slotted spoon and set aside to drain on kitchen paper. Serve immediately.

FISH HEAD SOUP SERVES 4-6

I know this sounds a bit odd, and if you're squeamish, please don't turn the page as it's worth a try. For me, all the flavour of the fish is in the head. Mum and I used to break the head in half and share it, and weirdly enough, I have a thing for eating the eyes and cheeks. I won't carry on, for fear you will close the book in protest, but believe me, this is one seriously tasty soup. You don't have to eat the head, just use it here for flavour – even though my mum and I think it is sacrilege not to eat it. Most of the time you can get fish heads from your fishmonger for free, or at a very cheap price.

2 tbsp olive oil
1kg mixed fish heads
1 onion, finely chopped
1 carrot, peeled and finely chopped
1–2 red bird's eye chillies,
    finely chopped
1 tbsp fennel seeds
1 tbsp coriander seeds
1 bay leaf
3 garlic cloves, finely chopped
5 sprigs of thyme

½ tsp ground turmeric
200ml white wine
1 tbsp tomato purée
½ x 400g tin chopped tomatoes
2 litres fish stock
500ml water
salt and freshly ground black pepper
1 tbsp mixed freshly chopped
    flat-leaf parsley and coriander
pinch of dried chilli flakes

1 Heat the oil in a large pan and gently fry the fish heads until browned, about 3 minutes on each side. Remove from the pan and set aside.

2 Into the same pan add the onion, carrot, chillies, fennel seeds, coriander seeds, bay leaf, garlic, thyme and turmeric and cook, stirring, for about 3 minutes. Add the white wine and simmer for about 3–4 minutes to cook out the alcohol.

3 Add the tomato purée and chopped tomatoes and cook for 10 minutes; then add the stock and water and continue cooking for 10 minutes. Add the fish heads and cook for a further 15–20 minutes. You don't want to overcook the fish heads as they will start to give the soup a bitter taste. Taste and adjust the seasoning.

4 Scatter over the chopped parsley and coriander and chilli flakes before serving.

SEA BASS WITH CORIANDER AND CHILLI SERVES 4

1 x 1kg whole sea bass,
　gutted and scaled
½ bunch fresh coriander, roughly
　chopped
2 red chillies, finely chopped
1 tbsp cumin seeds, toasted (see page 10)
2 tbsp extra-virgin olive oil
sea salt

FOR THE DRESSING
juice of 2 limes
1 tsp unrefined light muscovado
　sugar
1 tsp fish sauce
2 tbsp olive oil

1 Preheat the oven to 190°C/gas 5.

2 Clean the sea bass, wiping it inside and out with kitchen paper. Use a sharp knife to gently score the fish with 3–4 diagonal cuts on both sides. Stuff the inside of the fish with the fresh coriander.

3 Mix together the chillies, cumin seeds, olive oil and salt and rub this mixture all over the outside of the fish. Place the fish on a baking tray and bake in the oven for about 30 minutes. The skin should crisp up nicely as the fish is not covered.

4 Check if the fish is cooked – the flesh should be opaque and feel firm to the touch. Return to the oven for a further 5 minutes if necessary.

5 Meanwhile, whisk together the dressing ingredients. Once the fish is cooked, remove the fillets using two spoons and then drizzle a little dressing over each portion.

WRAPPED MONKFISH WITH COCONUT AND TOMATO SERVES 4

2 monkfish tails, about 375g each,
  skin and membrane removed
3cm piece of fresh root ginger,
  peeled and grated
2 garlic cloves, finely chopped
2 tbsp freshly chopped coriander stalks
1 tsp thyme leaves
1 tbsp rapeseed oil
2 tbsp olive oil
salt and freshly ground black pepper

FOR THE DRESSING
3 vine tomatoes, quartered and seeded
1 garlic clove
½ bunch fresh coriander
½ bunch fresh flat-leaf parsley
1 tbsp thyme leaves
1 red bird's eye chilli, chopped
3 tbsp desiccated coconut
2 tbsp rapeseed oil
½ tsp salt

1 Season the monkfish tails all over with salt and leave for an hour. Monkfish tails can release a milky juice when cooked, so salting beforehand removes some of this excess liquid. After an hour, rinse the fish and pat dry with kitchen paper. Preheat the oven to 190°C/gas 5.

2 To prepare the dressing, place all the dressing ingredients in a food processor and blitz until combined. Set aside.

3 Using a sharp knife, make a cut lengthways down each monkfish tail, taking care not to cut right the way through. Open the tail out a little and stuff the middle with the ginger, garlic, coriander stalks and thyme leaves. Roll up and tie with kitchen string. Rub the tails with rapeseed oil and season all over with salt and pepper.

4 Heat the olive oil in a large frying pan and when hot, add the monkfish tails. Brown on all sides for about 2 minutes to seal in all the juices.

5 Cut two pieces of foil, large enough to wrap each monkfish tail in. Place half the dressing in the centre of a piece of foil and place a monkfish tail on top. Bring up the sides of the foil and seal, leaving space inside the parcel for the fish to steam. Repeat with the other monkfish tail. Cook in the oven for 12–15 minutes (cooking times may vary depending on the size).

6 Unwrap the parcels and serve the monkfish with the wonderful warm dressing it has been roasted in.

SEARED LOBSTER WITH LIME AND CORIANDER BUTTER SERVES 4

2 x 1kg live lobsters (see Note)
3 tbsp olive oil
100g unsalted butter
1 large red chilli, finely chopped

juice of 3 limes
3 tbsp freshly chopped coriander
1 tbsp freshly chopped garlic chives
sea salt and freshly ground black pepper

1 In order to kill the lobsters humanely, place them in the freezer for a couple of hours – this will put them into a comatose state. The quickest way is then to plunge the tip of a sharp knife straight down behind the lobster's eyes. Slit the lobster lengthways and set aside.

2 Place a skillet or large frying pan over a high heat and wait for the pan to start smoking. Add the olive oil and place the lobster straight into the pan, flesh-side down.

3 Using tongs, move the lobster around to ensure all the sides are seared, this takes about 4 minutes on each side. The shell should turn a bright red and should start colouring the oil.

4 Reduce the heat to medium and then add the butter, chilli and salt and pepper and cook for 1 minute. Remove from heat, add the lime juice, coriander and garlic chives and leave to rest in the pan for a further 5 minutes. Serve warm. (Pictured on page 71.)

NOTE
You could also buy pre-cooked lobster and start the recipe from step 2. Please note that the lobster will need slightly less cooking in step 3 – about 2 minutes on each side.

KING PRAWNS WITH CHINESE SPINACH AND GARLIC SERVES 4

I love Chinese spinach as it's fresh and vibrant in colour, and releases a wonderful earthy tasting liquid when cooked. I leave the prawns whole as the heads and shells give the dish a lovely strong, sweet, prawn flavour.

2 tbsp vegetable oil
3 garlic cloves, finely sliced
2 bird's eye chillies, finely sliced
100g Chinese spinach (see Note), roughly chopped
16 large raw prawns, heads and shells left on

2 tbsp light soy sauce
1 tsp rice wine vinegar
2 whole dried red chillies, chopped
1 spring onion, finely chopped
2 tsp sesame oil

1 Heat the vegetable oil in a large pan over a medium heat and add the garlic. Allow to sizzle and turn light golden before adding the fresh chillies and Chinese spinach.

2 Add the prawns, soy sauce and rice wine vinegar and cook for 5 minutes. Sprinkle over the dried red chillies and chopped spring onion and drizzle with the sesame oil. Serve immediately with some steamed basmati rice (see page 144).

NOTE
Chinese spinach can be found in Asian supermarkets although you can use pak choy as an alternative.

MONKFISH AND AUBERGINE CURRY SERVES 4

This is my sister's all-time favourite curry. Whenever Mum asks her what she fancies for dinner, she always asks for this. At home, Mum uses whole red snapper, cutting the fish into thick slices with the bone in each slice. I've used monkfish, which has very few bones, so is a more child-friendly option as well as being easier for dinner party guests.

500g monkfish tail, skin and membrane removed
vegetable oil for frying
1 large aubergine, cut into 5cm cubes
1 onion, finely chopped
3 garlic cloves, grated on a microplane
2.5cm piece of fresh root ginger, peeled and grated on a microplane

1 bird's eye chilli, halved lengthways
10 curry leaves
3 tbsp Mauritian curry powder (see page 10)
3 tomatoes, roughly chopped
500ml fish stock
4 tbsp freshly chopped coriander
salt

1 Cut the monkfish fillet into 5cm pieces. Heat some vegetable oil in a large frying pan over a medium heat – you need a depth of about 2.5cm – and shallow-fry the fish pieces for around 2 minutes on each side. Drain on kitchen paper and set aside.

2 Shallow-fry the aubergine in the same oil until golden on all sides, drain on kitchen paper and set aside.

3 Add a little more oil to the pan and add the onions, garlic, ginger, chilli and curry leaves. Reduce the heat and cook until the onions are translucent, about 5 minutes.

4 Add the curry powder and allow the oil to turn yellow; add the tomatoes. Cook for 15 minutes, stirring, until completely dry. Add the fish stock, bring to the boil and simmer for 20 minutes. Season with salt.

5 Return the fish and aubergine to the pan and allow to heat through for a few minutes. Sprinkle with chopped coriander and serve.

CHILLI AND LIME SQUID

SERVES 4

---

3 medium whole squid,
  with tentacles, cleaned
2 tbsp olive oil
2 garlic cloves, finely sliced
juice of 1 lime
1 lime, quartered

2 tbsp freshly chopped
  coriander stalks
2 spring onions, finely chopped
1 whole red chilli, finely chopped
salt and freshly ground black
  pepper

---

1 Cut the squid tentacles into 3cm pieces and slice the bodies into rings.

2 Heat the oil in a large pan and when hot, add the squid. After a few seconds add all the remaining ingredients and cook for 4–5 minutes (don't overcook the squid or it will become tough).

3 Season with salt and white pepper and serve immediately.

CRAB, APPLE AND POMELO

SERVES 4

Pomelo is a beautiful fruit found throughout Asia. It looks like a grapefruit but the segments are bigger and the flavour is much sweeter than grapefruit. I could write a whole book on combining seafood and fruit, but I will save it for another time. I love this simple recipe as it is just an assembly of fresh citrussy fruits next to sweet crab. It's also a seriously impressive dinner party starter requiring very little effort – just make sure you use fresh crabmeat as tinned crab won't cut the mustard.

If you can't get hold of pomelo, you can use grapefruit instead but just a quarter of a grapefruit, as it is much more tart in flavour.

400g fresh white crabmeat
2 granny smith apples, cored,
   quartered and cut into
   very fine slices
80g bean sprouts
½ pomelo, segments broken apart
1 tbsp roughly chopped coriander leaves
1 red chilli, finely chopped (optional)

FOR THE DRESSING
juice of 4 limes
1 tsp red wine vinegar
4 tbsp rapeseed oil
salt and freshly ground black pepper

1 Place all the ingredients for the dressing in a mixing bowl and whisk until well combined. Add all the other ingredients to the bowl and toss together. Serve immediately.

MUSSELS WITH WATERMELON AND CHILLI SERVES 6

I know this may sound like an odd combination, but the sweetness of the watermelon tempers the chilli and perfectly matches the sweetness of the mussels. It's important to adjust the salt at the end of the dish as you don't want to overpower completely the subtle taste of the mussels.

1kg live mussels
½ onion
2 bird's eye red chillies, chopped
500g watermelon, seeded and
  cut into chunks

½ x 400g tin plum tomatoes
1 garlic clove
4 tbsp freshly chopped coriander
large pinch of salt

1 Clean the mussels well in cold water and remove the beards. Discard any mussels with broken shells or that do not close when firmly tapped with the back of a knife.

2 Place all the ingredients except the mussels and salt in a food processor and blitz until completely smooth. Transfer to a large, lidded pan and cook over a medium heat for 15 minutes. Keep stirring so the mixture doesn't stick to the bottom of the pan.

3 The mixture should start to thicken and darken in colour. Tip in the cleaned mussels, cover tightly with a lid and steam for 5 minutes. Discard any mussels that remain firmly closed; add salt to taste. Serve immediately with plenty of napkins – this is a messy dish!

STUFFED STEAMED SQUID SERVES 2

This is a really easy dish and will make your friends think you spent ages in the kitchen! It's quick to assemble and even quicker to cook, perfect for a night in for two.

1 large squid, including tentacles
150g cooked basmati rice
  (see page 144)
2 tbsp freshly chopped coriander stalks
1 tsp dried red chilli flakes
1 tsp ground cumin

salt and freshly ground black pepper
3 shallots, deep-fried (see page 11),
  to serve
2 large red chillies, seeded and
  roughly chopped, to serve
green salad, to serve

1 Thoroughly clean the squid by removing the sinewy skin, along with the quill (the bone in the middle) and the ink sack. Remove the tentacles, cut into small pieces and set aside. If this makes you squeamish just ask your fishmonger to do it for you.

2 Mix together the cooked rice with the chopped coriander stalks, chilli flakes, cumin, chopped tentacles and seasoning and use this rice mixture to stuff the body of the squid. Secure the end with a couple of toothpicks to keep the filling in.

3 Place a piece of parchment paper inside a bamboo steamer and steam the squid for 15 minutes.

4 To serve, slice the squid into circles revealing the rice stuffing and scatter with deep-fried shallots and chopped chillies. Enjoy with a simple green salad.

GRILLED SWORDFISH WITH POMEGRANATE SERVES 4

1 tsp hot paprika
1 tsp ground cumin
1 tsp ground coriander
2 tsp sumac
2 tbsp vegetable oil
4 swordfish steaks, about 170g each

salt
1 whole pomegranate, halved
juice of 1 lime
2 saffron threads
1 tbsp freshly chopped coriander
salt and freshly ground black pepper

1 Mix together the paprika, cumin, coriander, sumac and vegetable oil and rub this all over the swordfish steaks. Leave to rest in the fridge. After about 30 minutes remove from the fridge and season with salt.

2 Place a griddle pan over a high heat; when it starts smoking add the swordfish steaks. Cook them for around 3–4 minutes on each side, being careful not to overcook them – the fish should be still slightly pink and juicy on the inside.

3 Remove from the pan and then squeeze the juice and seeds from the pomegranate into the pan, along with the lime juice, saffron and salt and pepper. Cook until the liquid starts to reduce and become syrupy around the edges of the pan, about 2–3 minutes. Add the coriander at the last minute and then pour straight over the steaks.

4 This dish goes perfectly with Quinoa Pilau (see page 156).

THE GOODNESS OF THE LAND
MEAT

This chapter will take you through many different styles of cooking, from African-inspired Wild Boar Sausages in Creole Sauce to Sino-Mauritian Beef with Green Peppers, to the classic French daube and finally to the Indo-Mauritian influenced curries.

Venison, chicken, rabbit and hare are abundant in Mauritius but most of the lamb and beef eaten is imported from Australia. You will notice that a lot of the recipes call for the meat to be slow-cooked on top of a stove. Using an oven in Mauritius is quite rare, largely because of the way cooking has evolved on the island, from one large pot over a hot fire to a portable gas hob in the home. A lot of meals are prepared using a pressure cooker or a wok because these methods of cooking have a speedier cooking time and therefore preserve energy supplies.

CHICKEN FRICASSEE WITH SWEETCORN SERVES 4-6

450g skinless and boneless chicken
   thighs, cut into large chunks
2 tbsp olive oil
4 garlic cloves, finely chopped
2 tbsp finely chopped coriander
   stalks
8 sprigs of thyme, leaves picked

2 bay leaves
550ml chicken stock
2 corn cobs, kernels sliced off
1 banana shallot, thinly sliced
salt and freshly ground black pepper
fresh baguette or steamed basmati rice
   (see page 144), to serve

1 Season the chicken with salt and pepper. Heat the oil in a large pan over a medium heat and fry the chicken for 5 minutes, turning frequently, until evenly browned all over. Remove from the pan and set aside.

2 Add the garlic, coriander stalks, thyme and bay leaves to the pan and cook for 2–3 minutes until the garlic starts to colour. Return the chicken to the pan, pour over the stock and bring to a simmer. Reduce the heat, cover and cook for 20 minutes.

3 Add the sweetcorn kernels and cook for a further 5 minutes. Remove from the heat, taste and adjust the seasoning and scatter over the thinly sliced shallot. Serve with a fresh baguette or some steamed basmati rice.

CHICKEN AND CHINESE SPINACH

SERVES 4–6

2 tbsp vegetable oil
1 onion, thinly sliced
2 tsp Ginger and Garlic Paste
  (see page 11)
1 tsp finely chopped red chilli
350g skinless and boneless chicken
  thighs, cut into bite-sized pieces

2 tbsp oyster sauce
2 tbsp light soy sauce
½ tsp white pepper
300g Chinese spinach or pak choy
steamed basmati rice (see page 144),
  to serve
Mango Kutcha (see page 174), to serve

1 Heat the oil in a wok over a high heat until smoking. Add the onion,
ginger and garlic paste and chilli and stir-fry for 1 minute. Add the
chicken and cook for 4 minutes, until evenly browned on all sides.

2 Add the oyster sauce, soy sauce, white pepper and Chinese spinach
and cook for a further 2 minutes.

3 Serve with steamed rice and Mango Kutcha.

DAUBE DE BOEUF SERVES 4–5

Originating from the Daube region of France, this is a rich stew that is slow-cooked with wine and potatoes. In Mauritius we use more tomatoes than the original French version and slightly fewer ingredients. It's perfect served on a cold winter evening.

I prefer to cook this dish with the bone as it helps to build layers of flavour. The marrow also thickens the sauce and adds a gelatinous shine.

2 tbsp vegetable oil
1 large onion, finely chopped
4 garlic cloves, finely chopped
8 sprigs of thyme
3 bay leaves
2 red chillies, finely chopped
500g beef shank, with bone
250ml red wine

100ml dry sherry
1 x 400g tin plum tomatoes
200g potatoes, peeled and chopped
  into 2.5cm cubes
salt and freshly ground black pepper
fresh coriander and flat-leaf parsley,
  to garnish

1 Heat the oil in a large pan over a medium heat and fry the onion for a few minutes until translucent. Add the garlic, thyme, bay leaves and chillies and cook for a further 2 minutes.

2 Add the beef and bone and cook for about 5 minutes, turning frequently, until browned. Add the red wine, sherry and tomatoes and bring to a simmer. Reduce the heat, cover and cook for around 45 minutes. Season with salt and pepper then add the potato and cook for a further 25 minutes.

3 Remove the bone before serving and garnish with fresh parsley and coriander.

RS
12.00

162

CARI MUTTON SERVES 4-6

Mutton is a wonderfully rich meat that can handle a lot of spices and chilli really well. This is the dish that I cooked in the final of *MasterChef*: I never thought that one of our family's classic curries would be enough to secure me the title. It tastes even better the next day as all the spices harmonise and the flavours go deep into the meat.

3 tbsp vegetable oil
1 onion, finely chopped
5 garlic cloves, finely chopped
2.5cm piece of fresh root ginger, peeled and grated
2 red bird's eye chillies, finely chopped
12 curry leaves
4 tbsp Mauritian curry powder (see page 10)

½ tsp fenugreek seeds
500g mutton shoulder, chopped into 2.5cm cubes
1 x 400g tin plum tomatoes
300ml water
3 tbsp freshly chopped coriander, plus extra to garnish
salt and freshly ground white pepper

1 Heat the oil in a large pan over a medium heat and gently fry the onion, garlic, ginger and chillies until soft. Add the curry leaves, curry powder and fenugreek seeds and continue frying for 1 minute.

2 Add the mutton and cook for 15 minutes, turning frequently, until evenly browned on all sides, then add the tomatoes, water and coriander and bring to a simmer. Reduce the heat, cover and leave to simmer for 2½–3 hours, or until the mutton is tender. Alternatively, make this dish in a pressure cooker and cook for 1½ hours.

3 Taste and adjust the seasoning, garnish with more chopped coriander and serve.

CIVET DE CERF SERVES 6

This is a rich, subtly spiced one-pot dish of braised venison.

3 tbsp olive oil
2 Spanish onions, finely sliced
2 garlic cloves, finely sliced
1 cinnamon stick
1 tbsp fresh thyme leaves
4 cloves
1kg venison haunch, trimmed and cut
 into bite-sized chunks

2 medium tomatoes, quartered
125ml red wine
200ml beef stock
2 tbsp freshly chopped flat-leaf parsley
crusty bread or steamed basmati rice
 (see page 144), to serve

1 Heat the oil in a casserole over a medium heat and fry the onion for 5 minutes until lightly browned. Add the garlic, cinnamon stick, thyme and cloves and fry for 2 minutes.

2 Add the venison pieces and cook for about 10 minutes, until browned. Add the tomatoes and red wine and cook for a further 10 minutes.

3 Add the beef stock and bring to a simmer. Reduce the heat, cover and cook for 45–50 minutes, or until the venison is tender.

4 Sprinkle over the parsley and serve with crusty bread or steamed rice.

LAMB KALIA SERVES 4-6

I have fond memories of this as it was the dish my mum cooked the first time my husband was introduced to the family. Everyone's plates were wiped clean. This dish tastes better the longer you marinate the lamb so prepare the night before if you can.

2 tbsp vegetable oil
500g lamb shoulder,
   cut into bite-sized pieces
pinch of saffron strands
400ml hot water
2 medium potatoes, peeled and
   cut into bite-sized pieces
3 tbsp freshly chopped coriander
3 tbsp freshly chopped mint
salt

FOR THE MARINADE
3 garlic cloves, minced
1 onion, finely chopped
3 tsp ground cumin
3 tsp garam masala
2 dried red chillies
1 cinnamon stick
1 tsp ground turmeric
5 cardamom seeds, crushed
170g Greek-style yoghurt

1 Combine all the ingredients for the marinade in a large bowl. Add the lamb pieces and rub in the marinade, massaging it well so all the flavours start to penetrate into the meat. Cover with cling film and chill for at least 8 hours, or overnight.

2 Heat the oil in a large, non-stick pan over a medium heat. Add the lamb and cook for 5–10 minutes until browned. Add the saffron to the hot water, stir to dissolve and then add to the pan. Cover and cook for 40 minutes.

3 Add the potatoes and cook for a further 25 minutes. Add the coriander and mint, season with salt and serve.

TANDOORI CHICKEN SERVES 4

Typically this would be cooked in a tandoor or clay oven but this version is just cooked in an ordinary oven.

8 skinless chicken legs
1 tsp salt

FOR THE MARINADE
1 tbsp ground coriander
1 tbsp ground cumin
1 tsp ground turmeric
1 tbsp cayenne
1 tbsp garam masala
2 tbsp sweet paprika
200ml natural yoghurt
juice of 1 lemon
3 garlic cloves, finely minced

FOR THE RED RICE WITH THYME
300g steamed basmati rice
   (see page 144)
1 garlic clove, finely chopped
1 red chilli, finely chopped
½ x 400g tin chopped tomatoes
1 tsp salt
2 tbsp fresh thyme leaves

1 Place all the marinade ingredients in a mixing bowl and stir to combine.

2 Place the chicken legs into a dish and slash the meat a few times each to create grooves. Rub the marinade into the chicken, ensuring it gets right into the grooves to enable it to permeate through the meat. Cover with clingfilm and chill for at least 2–3 hours, or overnight.

3 Preheat the oven to 190°C/gas 5. Transfer the chicken to a baking sheet and cook in the oven for 45 minutes, or until cooked through.

4 Meanwhile, make the red rice. Prepare the basmati rice according to the recipe on page 146.

5 Place the garlic, red chilli, tomatoes and salt into a large pan and cook over a medium heat for about 5–10 minutes. Remove from the heat then add the cooked rice and thyme leaves.

WILD BOAR SAUSAGES IN CREOLE SAUCE SERVES 4

This is one of my brother's favourite recipes. Whenever my mum got hold of these sausages, she would make this delicious spicy Creole sauce to go with them.

1 tbsp olive oil
8 wild boar sausages
2 banana shallots, finely chopped
3 garlic cloves, minced
½ tsp dried chilli

6 sprigs of thyme, leaves picked,
    plus extra to garnish
1 x 400g tin plum tomatoes
1 tbsp tomato purée
salt

1 Heat the oil in a large frying pan over a medium to high heat and fry the sausages for 5–10 minutes until evenly browned all over.

2 Remove the sausages from the pan and set aside. Add the shallots and sauté for a few minutes until softened, then add the garlic, chilli and thyme and cook for a further 2 minutes.

3 Add the tomatoes and tomato purée and bring to a simmer. Reduce the heat to medium, cover and cook for 20 minutes. Return the sausages to the pan and cook for a further 15 minutes.

4 Season with salt, sprinkle with fresh thyme leaves and serve.

OXTAIL WITH BUTTER BEANS

SERVES 6-8

Whenever I cook this dish I think of my friends Louise and Jerry as they make it every year at their annual party. It's a great dish for entertaining as you can prepare it in the morning, or even the night before. Oxtail is a fantastic cut of meat: dark and rich with plenty of flavour. This is a firm favourite of mine as I love meat that falls off the bone and butter beans are one of my all-time top pulses.

3 tbsp vegetable oil
1 onion, roughly chopped
3 garlic cloves
4 sprigs of thyme
1kg oxtail, cut into bite-sized pieces
    (ask your butcher to do this for you)
2 medium tomatoes, roughly chopped

1 litre vegetable stock
1 x 400g tin butter beans, drained
salt and freshly ground black pepper

TO GARNISH
1 tbsp sliced spring onion tips
2 tbsp freshly chopped flat-leaf parsley

1 Heat the oil in a large pan over a medium heat and fry the onion with the garlic and thyme for 3–4 minutes, or until beginning to soften. Add the oxtail and cook for 5 minutes until evenly browned on all sides.

2 Add the tomatoes and vegetable stock, season with black pepper and bring to a simmer. Reduce the heat, cover and cook for 40 minutes. Add the butter beans, season with salt and cook for a further 25 minutes.

3 Garnish with the spring onion tips and parsley and serve.

GOAT HALIM SERVES 4-6

Halim is a typical Mauritian meal that is very popular during the month of Ramadan as it is really hearty with protein from the meat and the pulses, and is perfect when fasting or on cold winter nights. Persian in origin, this has been adapted in the true Creole style and is usually served topped with chopped cucumber, chilli, spring onion and coriander, alongside a crusty French baguette.

My cousin Devina makes an incredible *halim* – the last time we visited her she made us a fantastic vegetarian version. Try substituting the meat with fried aubergine batons or brown lentils.

2 tbsp vegetable oil
700g goat meat, chopped into
   bite-sized pieces
1 onion, chopped
5 garlic cloves, crushed
2 tbsp toasted cumin seeds
   (see page 10)
2 green cardamom pods, crushed
1 tsp ground turmeric
1 cinnamon stick
1 tsp freshly ground black pepper
1 tsp hot chilli powder

2 tbsp garam masala
200g yellow lentils, washed
2 litres vegetable stock
2 tbsp freshly chopped coriander
2 tbsp freshly chopped mint
crusty French baguette, to serve

TO GARNISH
chopped cucumber
sliced fresh chilli
freshly chopped coriander
sliced spring onion

1 Heat the oil in a large casserole over a medium heat and fry the goat pieces for 3–4 minutes, until evenly browned on all sides. Remove the meat and set aside. Add the onion and garlic to the same pan and cook for 3 minutes, until just beginning to brown.

2 Add all of the spices and then return the meat to the pan. Add the lentils, pour over the stock and bring to a simmer. Reduce the heat, cover and cook for 1 hour. Add the coriander and mint and simmer for a further 15 minutes.

3 Garnish with cucumber, chilli, coriander and spring onions, and serve with a crusty warm French baguette.

CHINESE-STYLE BEEF WITH GREEN PEPPERS SERVES 4

1 tbsp cornflour
1 tbsp light soy sauce
1 tbsp oyster sauce
1 tbsp rice wine vinegar
250g beef tenderloin, thinly sliced
2 tbsp groundnut oil

3 garlic cloves, finely sliced
1 large green chilli, finely chopped
1 large green pepper, seeded
  and diced
2 spring onions, finely chopped
freshly ground white pepper

1 Combine the cornflour, soy sauce, oyster sauce and vinegar together in a bowl and season with white pepper. Place the beef in a shallow dish and pour over the marinade. Mix well to coat the beef, cover with cling film and chill for 20 minutes.

2 Heat the oil in a wok over a high heat until smoking. Add the beef and stir-fry for 2 minutes. Remove the beef and set aside. Add the garlic, chilli and pepper to the wok and stir-fry for 3 minutes, or until the peppers are just softened, adding a little water if the wok becomes dry.

3 Return the beef to the wok and toss together for 30 seconds. Remove from the heat, sprinkle with the spring onions and serve.

BEEF AND GREEN PAPAYA CURRY SERVES 4-5

Green papaya works really well with beef as the natural enzymes
that exist in papaya tenderise the meat as it cooks, helping to make
it deliciously soft.

2 tbsp vegetable oil
400g beef shin, cut into bite-sized pieces
1 shallot, finely chopped
3 garlic cloves, minced
8 curry leaves
2 green chillies, halved lengthways
3 tbsp Mauritian curry powder
  (see page 10)

1 litre vegetable stock
½ large green papaya,
  cut into 2.5cm cubes

TO GARNISH
freshly chopped coriander
fried curry leaves (optional)

1 Heat the oil in a large pan over a medium heat and cook the beef for
5 minutes, turning frequently, until evenly browned on all sides. Remove
the beef from the pan and set aside.

2 Add the shallot, garlic, curry leaves and chillies to the pan and cook
for 3 minutes. Add the curry powder, browned beef and stock and bring
to a simmer. Reduce the heat, cover and cook for 45 minutes, stirring
occasionally to make sure the curry doesn't stick to the bottom of the pan.

3 Add the papaya and cook, covered, for a further 45 minutes, until the
beef is meltingly tender.

4 Sprinkle over the fresh coriander, top with a few fried curry leaves,
if liked, and serve immediately.

VARIATION
To make a pork and jackfruit curry, use 400g pork tenderloin instead
of the beef shin, and half a medium jackfruit instead of the papaya.

LAPIN A LA POIS SERVES 4-6

Rabbit is cooked a lot in Mauritius and is definitely part of France's culinary legacy. This dish is also cooked using hare, which is plentiful on the island. It's a beautiful dish and was, in fact, one of my dad's favourites. (To be honest, anything that included peas seemed to be my dad's favourite.)

2 tbsp olive oil
1 onion, finely chopped
3 bay leaves
4 sprigs of thyme
4 garlic cloves, finely chopped
2 green chillies, halved lengthways
500g rabbit pieces

175ml dry white wine
500ml vegetable stock
200g garden peas, fresh or frozen

TO GARNISH
freshly chopped parsley
freshly snipped garlic chives

1 Heat the oil in a casserole over a medium heat and fry the onion with the bay leaves and thyme for 2 minutes. Add the garlic and chillies and cook for a further 2 minutes.

2 Add the rabbit pieces and cook for 5 minutes, turning frequently, until evenly browned all over. Add the wine and cook until completely evaporated.

3 Add the stock and bring to a simmer. Reduce the heat, cover and cook for 45 minutes, or until the rabbit is tender. About 5 minutes before the end of the cooking time, add the peas. Sprinkle with the parsley and chives and serve.

PORK AND LIME SERVES 4

This was one of the dishes taught to me by the chef and writer David Thompson in Thailand. This version has been simplified and uses ingredients that are readily available outside Thailand. The taste should be hot, salty, sour and sweet all at once. A delicious party staple, or perfect to ward off an approaching cold!

300g pork neck fillet or tenderloin
2 garlic cloves, finely chopped
1 tsp galangal, grated
  (or use fresh root ginger)
2 bird's eye chillies, seeded and
  chopped
1 lemon grass stalk, trimmed and
  finely chopped
3 tbsp finely chopped coriander stalks
1 tbsp vegetable oil

1 tsp shrimp paste
2 tbsp fish sauce
juice of 3 limes and segments of 1
1 tbsp brown sugar
70g green beans, sliced
5 spring onions, sliced
handful of fresh mint leaves
handful of fresh basil
steamed basmati rice (see page 144),
  to serve

1 Using a heavy knife, chop the pork into small pieces, then chop vigorously to form mince. This is a Thai technique to turn good-quality meat into mince. You can just use pork mince but the quality won't be as good.

2 In a pestle and mortar, lightly pound together the garlic, galangal, chillies, lemon grass and coriander to form a rough paste. Heat the oil in a wok over a high heat, add the garlic mixture and pork and cook for 3–4 minutes, until the pork is cooked through.

3 Add the shrimp paste, fish sauce, lime juice, lime segments and sugar and cook for a further minute. Add the beans and spring onions and cook for 2–3 minutes. Remove from the heat and toss through the fresh mint and basil leaves.

4 Serve with steamed basmati rice.

CHICKEN SURPRISE SERVES 2–4

One day, my uncle was babysitting my brother and me and he made a dish that he called 'chicken surprise'. Hilariously, the dish had no chicken in it, but was in fact stuffed cabbage leaves! My brother and I were admittedly very young, but apparently we tucked into the dish, clearing our plates, proclaiming it was the 'best chicken dish EVER'. My uncle was in hysterics and felt god-like, being able to turn cabbage into chicken. This dish does contain chicken but it still has the flavourings and spices included in the original recipe back in the 1980s. I've named it Chicken Surprise in honour of my uncle.

4 skinless chicken legs
¼ white cabbage, thinly sliced
1 red and 1 yellow pepper,
    seeded and thinly sliced
½ white onion, thinly sliced
2 garlic cloves, finely chopped
2 tsp garam masala

1 tbsp ground cumin
1 tbsp ground coriander
½ tsp ground turmeric
½ tsp salt
½ tsp white pepper
1 tbsp sunflower oil
2 sprigs of thyme

1 Preheat the oven to 160°C/gas 2½.

2 Slash the chicken legs a few times to allow the spices to penetrate the meat during cooking and then place in a large roasting tin. Add the cabbage, peppers, onion and garlic and toss together so everything is combined.

3 Mix together all of the dry spices then add them to the pan, together with the salt, white pepper, oil and thyme sprigs. Make sure all the vegetables and chicken legs are evenly coated in the spices and then roast in the oven for 1 hour.

4 Serve with the Fresh Carrot Salad (see page 139).

CHICKEN HEART TOUFE SERVES 4-6

The idea of cooking with chicken hearts may turn some people off but I really wanted to include this as I firmly believe in nose-to-tail eating. Offal features heavily in Mauritian cooking because Mauritians' frugal nature means they don't want to waste any part of the animal. Ask your butcher for chicken hearts or look online for a supplier.

1 tbsp oil
300g chicken hearts
½ tsp white pepper
¼ tsp salt

½ tsp hot chilli powder
1 tsp sweet paprika
steamed basmati rice (see page 144)
or warm crusty bread, to serve

1 Heat the oil in a frying pan over a medium to high heat and add the chicken hearts, followed by all the remaining ingredients. Cook for about 7 minutes. Take care not to overcook the hearts, as they will become chewy, dry and tough – if they start to ooze liquid then you need to remove them from the heat.

2 Serve with steamed basmati rice or with warm crusty bread as part of *gajaks* before a main meal.

SPICY KEBABS MAKES 12-14 SKEWERS

These simple and easy-to-prepare kebabs are perfect to make ahead
of time for a barbecue.

400g minced lamb
2 green chillies, finely chopped
2 garlic cloves, finely chopped
1 tbsp ground cumin
1 tbsp hot paprika
2 tbsp garam masala
1 egg

2 tbsp freshly chopped mint
2 tbsp freshly chopped coriander
100g cooked yellow lentils, blitzed
   to a fine paste in a food processor
sunflower oil, for drizzling
lemon wedges, to serve
salt and freshly ground black pepper

1 In a bowl, mix all of the ingredients except the oil and lemon wedges
together until well combined. Chill in the fridge for at least 2 hours,
or overnight if possible.

2 Preheat the oven to 220°C/gas 7 or fire up the barbecue.

3 Shape the meat mixture around metal skewers to form kebabs. Drizzle
over a little oil and place on a roasting tray, so that the skewers are resting
on the sides of the tray and the kebabs themselves are suspended over the
tray. Alternatively, place directly on the barbecue.

4 Cook for 15–20 minutes, depending on how you like your lamb cooked,
and serve with lemon wedges.

ALL THINGS GREEN AND GOOD

VEGETABLES

One of the best things about Mauritian food, in my opinion, is the sheer variety of vegetables, pulses and greens that are used in every dish. A meal isn't complete without a vegetarian side dish or two, and the salads are so delicious that you probably wouldn't even notice that you didn't have any meat in your meal.

When I was a child vegetables were a staple at every mealtime. They were never hidden and were often the star of the dish, from stewed cabbage to okra, to the famous Mauritian Creole sauce rougaille. Vegetables are seen not only as an accompaniment to a meal, but a meal in themselves.

In Mauritius, typical vegetables include a range of bredes, which are basically green leaves such as cabbage, taro and pumpkin leaves, along with patty pan squash, cho-cho, okra, margose (bitter cucumber), aubergines and lots of fresh salads, tomatoes and cucumbers. There is a thriving Hindi community on the island, and many of them are vegetarian, so there is a real range and diversity of vegetable dishes prepared.

This chapter is probably my favourite as I love transforming simple vegetables into delicious, heart-warming meals. I hope I can inspire you to cook more with vegetables.

WHITE CABBAGE WITH CANNELLINI BEANS SERVES 4–6

White cabbage tends to get neglected, usually used only for coleslaw, and is often found at the back of the fridge, a day or two past its best. However, I think white cabbage is glorious.

I love this dish as the natural sweetness of the cabbage works so well with the subtle spices. Although this is essentially a side dish, the addition of cannellini beans adds extra depth and makes it a great lunch served with a wholemeal pitta bread.

1 tbsp sunflower oil
1 Spanish onion, finely chopped
1 tsp cumin seeds
1 tsp fennel seeds
1 tsp white pepper
1 white cabbage, finely chopped

1 x 400g tin cannellini beans, drained and rinsed
olive oil, for drizzling
freshly chopped flat-leaf parsley, to garnish
salt

1 Heat the sunflower oil in a large, lidded casserole over a medium to low heat. Add the onion, cumin seeds, fennel seeds and white pepper and season with salt. Cook for 5 minutes, until the onions are translucent and you can smell the wonderful aroma being released from the spices.

2 Add the cabbage, stir and immediately cover with the lid. Cook for 10 minutes, stirring every couple of minutes.

3 Add the cannellini beans and cook for a further 10 minutes – the cabbage should be wilted and translucent. Drizzle over a little olive oil, sprinkle with the parsley and serve hot.

AUBERGINE TOUFE SERVES 2-3

Toufé in Creole roughly translates as 'fry and steam', and you can cook pretty much any vegetable in this way. At first it seems like you're frying them, but the vegetables end up steaming in their own liquid, which is a wonderful way to cook them. Aubergine *toufé* goes with most things, but I think it's delicious on top of toasted Italian bread that has been rubbed with olive oil and garlic. Perhaps not what a Mauritian would do, but this is definitely what happens in my household.

2 tbsp olive oil
2 garlic cloves, thinly sliced
2 medium aubergines, sliced into
　matchsticks

1 tbsp freshly picked thyme leaves
2 small dried bird's eye chillies,
　crushed
salt

1 Heat the oil in a large frying pan with a tight-fitting lid over a medium heat. Add the garlic and cook for 1 minute. Add the aubergines, thyme and chillies and season with salt.

2 Move the aubergine matchsticks around the pan to ensure they are seasoned well and the oil is evenly distributed, then cover, reduce the heat to low and cook for 20 minutes, stirring gently after 10 minutes.

3 Serve with fresh Roti (see page 159) and Satchini Coco (see page 168).

CHICKPEA AND POTATO CURRY

SERVES 6

1 tsp fennel seeds
1 tsp cumin seeds
1 tbsp vegetable oil
2 shallots, finely chopped
2 garlic cloves, crushed
2 fresh green chillies, pierced
  with a knife but left whole
1 x 400g tin peeled plum tomatoes
2 tbsp Mauritian curry powder
  (see page 10)
1 x 400g tin chickpeas, rinsed
  and drained

2 medium potatoes, peeled and
  chopped into 2.5cm cubes
1 cinnamon stick
½ tsp unrefined brown sugar
salt
Dal Puri (see page 162),
  to serve

TO GARNISH
2 tbsp Greek-style yoghurt
freshly chopped coriander

1 Heat a frying pan over a high heat and lightly toast the fennel and cumin seeds for 2–3 minutes. Add the oil, shallots, garlic and whole chillies – the idea is to get the flavour from the chillies without the heat. Cook for 1 minute; then add the tomatoes and curry powder. Cook for 15 minutes, stirring occasionally.

2 Reduce the heat to medium to low and add the chickpeas, potatoes, cinnamon stick and sugar and pour over 200ml of water. Cook for 30 minutes until the potatoes are cooked all the way through and the tip of a knife can be inserted easily.

3 Season with salt, garnish with yoghurt and coriander and serve with fresh Dal Puri.

POTATO AND KIDNEY BEAN DAUBE SERVES 4-6

I love every kind of *daube* (the Mauritian version of stew). Traditionally from the Daube region of France, these stews have become a staple in every Mauritian household. My version with potatoes and kidney beans is a very simple dish using only a handful of ingredients. I love eating this with steamed basmati rice and Fresh Carrot Salad (see pages 144 and 139), but you could probably eat this on its own and not feel underfed.

2 tbsp rapeseed oil
2 small banana shallots, thinly sliced
1 garlic clove, finely chopped
2 tbsp freshly chopped coriander stalks
1 green chilli, finely chopped
1 tsp salt
4 sprigs of thyme
1 x 400g tin peeled plum tomatoes, use only half of the tomatoes but all of the juice

2 medium King Edward potatoes, or any non-chalky floury potato, chopped into 2.5 cm cubes
1 x 400g tin kidney beans, rinsed and drained
freshly chopped coriander, to garnish

1 Heat the oil in a large pan over a medium heat and fry the shallots for 2 minutes until just beginning to soften. Add the garlic, coriander, chilli, salt and thyme and cook for a further 2 minutes.

2 Add the tomatoes and cook for 5 minutes, stirring occasionally, then add the tomato juice and 200ml of water along with the potatoes and kidney beans. Bring to a simmer, reduce the heat, cover and cook for 15 minutes until the tomatoes start to break down (you can help this process along by using a wooden spoon to crush them).

3 Sprinkle over the coriander and serve hot.

SPICY QUINOA SALSA SERVES 6-8

My friend Keri absolutely loves quinoa and lives on the stuff. It's a wonderful grain from South America that is prized for its health benefits and is a great substitute for rice and pasta. On its own, quinoa is actually quite bland but it takes on other flavours beautifully. This is a great dish to take to a barbecue as it goes well with any grilled meat or fish. You can make it well in advance and dress the salad just before serving: it's guaranteed to impress. The key to success is to make sure the vegetables are evenly diced, then it's just an assembly job.

200g quinoa, cooked according to the packet instructions

100g brown lentils, cooked according to the packet instructions

1 jalapeño pepper, seeded and finely diced

1 red pepper, seeded and finely diced

1 yellow pepper, seeded and finely diced

3 spring onions, green parts only, finely diced

2 tomatoes, skinned, seeded and finely diced

100g sweetcorn, drained and rinsed

1 small red onion, finely chopped

FOR THE DRESSING

4 tbsp rapeseed oil

juice of 2 limes

1 tsp sweet paprika

1 tsp ground cumin

1 tsp salt

1 tsp white pepper

1 garlic clove, finely chopped

1 To make the dressing, place all the ingredients in a jam jar and shake thoroughly until completely combined.

2 Place all the remaining ingredients into a large bowl and pour the dressing over. Mix well to combine and serve.

LALO SERVES 3

Lalo is the Mauritian name for okra or 'lady's fingers'. Many people don't like the texture of okra as it becomes quite gluey when cooked for too long. This recipe keeps the okra fresh and light and I have added some zingy flavours to give it a real lift.

150g fresh okra, trimmed
1 banana shallot, finely chopped
4 tomatoes, skinned, seeded and
   finely chopped
1–2 green chillies, finely chopped
3 spring onions, finely chopped

2 tbsp freshly chopped coriander
   stalks
1 tbsp snipped fresh garlic chives
juice of 1 lime
1–2 tbsp olive oil
salt and freshly ground black pepper

1 Bring a large pan of salted water to the boil and put the okra in to cook for 2 minutes. Drain and plunge into ice-cold water. Set aside.

2 Place all the remaining ingredients except for the lime juice and olive oil in a large bowl and mix together. Drain the okra, slice into small rounds and add to the bowl.

3 Dress the salad with the lime juice and olive oil, being sure to coat all the vegetables and herbs, then season and serve. This goes well with Sea Bass with Coriander and Chilli (see page 66).

BREDE SONGES SERVES 3

My Aunty Devianee always asks me what I would like to have when I come to hers for dinner, I always say the same thing - Brede Songes and Rougaille. Her Brede Songes is always so delicious and is something I crave a lot when I am in the UK. This dish of Mauritian greens is traditionally made using taro leaves. If I had to choose my last supper, *brede songes* would definitely form part of it. You can order taro leaves online, or if you are lucky you might find them in Asian supermarkets. If you are struggling to find them, you can easily substitute with Swiss chard, including the stalks, which should be cooked in the same way to get the right finish for the dish. This is fantastic served with Egg Rougaille (see page 131) and fresh, hot *Roti* bread (see page 159). My idea of the perfect dinner.

1 tbsp vegetable oil
3 garlic cloves, finely chopped
2 medium tomatoes, finely chopped
1 tbsp tamarind paste

300g taro leaves (see Note) or
   Swiss chard, roughly chopped
salt

1 Heat the oil in a large wok over a medium heat and fry the garlic for 1 minute. Add the tomatoes and tamarind paste and cook for 3–4 minutes until the pan starts to dry out.

2 Add the taro leaves along with 100ml of hot water. Cook for 50 minutes, stirring occasionally, until the leaves are dark in colour and have formed a thick paste. Add more hot water as needed to prevent the mixture from drying out.

3 Season with salt and serve.

NOTE
If you are using taro leaves, please wear gloves to handle them as they tend to stain the hands dark purple. I've fallen foul of this on many occasions!

FAVA BEAN SOUP WITH CUMIN SERVES 6

This is not a Mauritian dish but I absolutely fell in love with it when I went to Morocco. The original dish is called *bessara* and is made using dried fava or broad beans. You'll find these in North African and Persian supermarkets.

300g dried fava beans, soaked
   overnight, drained and rinsed
2 litres vegetable stock
6 garlic cloves
1 tbsp hot smoked paprika
1 tbsp ground cumin, plus extra
   to serve

1 tsp white pepper
lemon juice, to taste
4 tbsp extra-virgin olive oil
1 tbsp freshly chopped coriander
salt

1 Place the fava beans in a large casserole and pour over the stock. Add the garlic cloves, cover and cook over a medium heat for 50 minutes.

2 Transfer the mixture to a blender or food processor in batches and blend until completely smooth.

3 Pour the mixture back into the casserole, return to the heat and add the paprika, cumin and white pepper. Stir and cook, uncovered, for a further 15 minutes.

4 Add lemon juice and salt to taste, then stir through the olive oil. Sprinkle with the coriander, add a pinch of cumin and serve.

MAURITIAN POTATO SALAD

SERVES 8

This salad is a staple at any Shelina bash or Permalloo party; I promise you, it's the best potato salad you'll ever eat. It's my friend Athar's favourite and he always gets me to make it when he comes for dinner so that he can take away the leftovers at the end of the night. It's been adapted over the years as the original recipe contained beetroot, which tends to turn the whole dish pink. I decided to leave out the beetroot and add a few extras of my own. So while this might not be a classic Mauritian potato salad, it is a salad that all your friends will love.

6 medium King Edward potatoes, about 400g, unpeeled
4 carrots, unpeeled
4 large eggs
4 spring onions, finely chopped

50ml olive oil
2 tbsp white wine vinegar
3 tbsp good-quality mayonnaise
2 tsp freshly ground black pepper
1½ tsp salt

1 Place the whole potatoes and carrots in a large pan of water over a high heat and bring to the boil. Reduce the heat, cover and simmer for 10 minutes, then add the eggs and simmer for a further 15 minutes. Carefully remove the eggs with a slotted spoon and set aside. Drain the potatoes and carrots and leave to cool.

2 Peel the potatoes, carrots and hard-boiled eggs. Cut the potatoes and carrots into 1-cm slices and slice or quarter the eggs lengthways. Place in a large serving bowl and sprinkle over the spring onions.

3 Mix together the remaining ingredients in a bowl and then add to the potatoes, carrots and eggs. Mix gently, being careful not to break up the eggs and potatoes too much. Serve immediately or chill for up to 2 days.

BUTTER BEAN CURRY SERVES 4

When I cooked this at the BBC Good Food Show in a cook-off against the previous year's *MasterChef* winner, Tim Anderson, it went down a treat with John Torode and Gregg Wallace. Tim asked me for the recipe some time afterwards as he said he had been craving my butter bean curry. I was hugely flattered. This is a typical street food dish, which is usually served-up alongside a *Dal Puri* (see page 162) and some hot and fiery coriander chutney. Street vendors wrap it in paper or foil and it's so delicious that you usually finish it before you've even left the stall; then you can't resist having another one.

2 tbsp vegetable oil
1 large white onion, finely chopped
3 garlic cloves, grated
2.5 cm piece of fresh root ginger, peeled and grated
5 curry leaves
3 tbsp Mauritian curry powder (see page 10)
2 red bird's eye chillies, roughly chopped

2 medium tomatoes, quartered
2 tbsp tomato purée
400ml hot water
1 x 400g tin butter beans, including the water from the tin
1 tbsp salt
freshly chopped coriander, to garnish
Roti (see page 159), to serve
Satchini Pomme d'Amour (see page 166), to serve

1 Heat the oil in a pan over a medium heat and fry the onion until translucent. Add the garlic, ginger and curry leaves and sauté for 3 minutes. Add the curry powder, chillies, tomatoes and tomato purée and cook for 5 minutes until thickened.

2 Add the hot water and butter beans along with the water from the tin and cook for 15 minutes, or until the sauce starts to thicken again. Season with salt.

3 Garnish with the coriander and serve with Roti and Satchini Pomme d'Amour. Delicious!

BLACK LENTIL FRICASSEE SERVES 4-6

When my sister was pregnant with my nephew, Rohan, my mum used to make this iron-rich dish for her to boost her energy. This typical French-influenced Mauritian dish has been adapted over the years with the introduction of fresh chilli and, usually, ginger. I leave out the ginger as I find that it overpowers the delicate flavour of the black lentils.

2 tbsp vegetable oil
1 large Spanish onion, finely chopped
2 garlic cloves, finely chopped
2 tbsp fresh thyme leaves, plus extra to garnish
2 green chillies, finely chopped

2 fresh bay leaves
250g puy lentils
1.5 litres vegetable stock
3 medium carrots, peeled and finely chopped
dried chilli flakes, to garnish
salt and freshly ground black pepper

1 Heat the oil in a large casserole over a medium heat and fry the onions until translucent. Add the garlic, thyme, chillies, bay leaves, puy lentils and stock and cook for 40–50 minutes.

2 Add the carrots, season with salt and pepper and cook, covered, for a further 25 minutes.

3 Serve hot garnished with thyme leaves and dried chilli flakes.

GREEN MANGO SALAD SERVES 3-4

Green (unripe) mango has such a different taste to ripe mango; slightly sour and bitter but still with an undeniable mango fragrance. This salad is perfect in hot weather; the sweet, salty, sour and hot flavours excite the taste buds. It works well with Spicy Aubergine Baja (see page 19).

70g cashew nuts
2 firm, unripe mangoes,
    peeled and stoned
1 large carrot
100g beansprouts
4 spring onions, finely sliced
1 tbsp freshly chopped mint
1 tbsp freshly chopped coriander stalks

FOR THE DRESSING
1 bird's eye chilli, finely chopped
1 garlic clove, finely chopped
2 tsp fish sauce or light soy sauce
1 tbsp molasses sugar
1 tbsp sesame oil
juice of 1 lime

1 Heat a frying pan over a high heat and toast the cashew nuts, then set aside to cool.

2 Using a mandolin, julienne the mango and carrot, or cut into thin matchsticks with a sharp knife. Place in a serving bowl with the beansprouts, spring onions, mint and coriander.

3 To make the dressing, whisk all the ingredients together in a jug and pour over the salad. Mix well and serve topped with the toasted cashew nuts.

CARI DES OEUFS SERVES 6

This traditional Creole dish, an egg and pea curry, takes me back to being a child when fresh meat and fish were a rare treat due to their expense. The dish has plenty of protein from the eggs and the sweetness of the peas complements the heat perfectly. *Cari des oeufs* really reminds me of my dad as he used to make it for us all the time. The strange thing is that I didn't like it that much when I was young but I realise that my parents made it for us as it was so nutritionally balanced. It was a cheap way of getting out protein and vegetables and is a classic example of the frugal nature of Mauritian cuisine.

2 tbsp vegetable oil
1 large Spanish onion
8 curry leaves
2 green chillies, finely chopped
3 garlic cloves, minced
3 tbsp Mauritian curry powder
  (see page 10)
1 tsp cumin seeds

1 tsp fenugreek seeds
2 medium tomatoes, chopped
1 tsp tomato purée
200g frozen petits pois
300ml water
5 large eggs, hard-boiled and peeled
2 tbsp freshly chopped coriander stalks
salt

1 Heat the oil in a pan over a medium heat and add the onion, curry leaves, chillies and garlic and sauté for 2–3 minutes until fragrant and aromatic.

2 Add the curry powder, cumin seeds and fenugreek seeds and cook for a further 2–3 minutes. Add the tomatoes and tomato purée and cook for 10 minutes.

3 Add the petits pois, pour over the water and cook for a further 10 minutes. Add the eggs and cook for a further 5 minutes to warm them through. Season with salt, garnish with the coriander stalks and serve.

EGG ROUGAILLE SERVES 2–3

Rougaille is a classic Creole sauce which gives its name to many Mauritian dishes; it looks like a simple tomato sauce but is so much more. It has a huge depth of flavour thanks to the European herbs parsley and thyme, the heat provided by the chilli and the Indian flavourings of ginger, coriander and garlic. It's truly divine and is my favourite sauce to prepare.

When I cook this dish I always think of my friend Krystle; we ate this dish a lot when we were at university together. With some rice and a salad, this got us through many hours of study, not to mention the occasional party.

3 tbsp vegetable oil
1 medium onion, finely chopped
2.5cm piece of fresh root ginger, peeled and grated
2 garlic cloves, grated
1 red bird's eye chilli, finely chopped

4 sprigs of thyme
1 x 400g tin peeled plum tomatoes
2 tbsp freshly chopped coriander
3 large eggs
freshly chopped flat-leaf parsley, to garnish
salt

1 Heat the vegetable oil in a large pan with a tight-fitting lid over a medium heat and fry the onion until just beginning to brown. Add the ginger, garlic, chilli and thyme and cook for 3–4 minutes, stirring occasionally.

2 Add the tomatoes and cook for 20–25 minutes until the tomatoes are beginning to break down and the oil has started to rise to the top of the mixture. Season with salt, add the chopped coriander and stir.

3 Crack the eggs into the pan, cover and cook for 5 minutes, or until the eggs are softly poached. Garnish with the parsley and serve. (Pictured on page 133.)

SQUASH AND MUSTARD FRICASSEE

SERVES 4–6

This usually makes up part of a dish called Seven Curries, which is a traditional dish eaten at weddings and celebrations. The dishes that make up the Seven Curries tend to be vegetarian and typically include a *rougaille*, a pumpkin curry, a potato curry, *Brede Songes* (see page 122) and spicy pickles, all served on a single banana leaf.

2 tbsp olive oil
1 garlic clove, finely chopped
2.5-cm piece of fresh root ginger, peeled and finely chopped
1 large dried red chilli
1 tbsp black mustard seeds

1 tbsp yellow mustard seeds
8 curry leaves
1 ambercup (onion) squash, peeled, seeded and cut into 2.5cm cubes
salt and freshly ground black pepper

1 Heat the oil in a large, heavy-based pan over a high heat. Add the garlic, ginger and whole dried chilli and fry for 2 minutes until fragrant. Add the mustard seeds and curry leaves and cook for a further minute.

2 Add the squash and reduce the heat. Cook for 30 minutes until the squash is softened and cooked through, stirring every 10 minutes to stop the squash sticking to the bottom of the pan. If it starts looking a little dry, add a tablespoon of water and cover.

3 Season with salt and pepper and serve.

RASON HOT AND SPICY MAURITIAN SOUP SERVES 6-8

This soup is similar to a *tom yum* soup (Thai hot and sour soup). It seems to have a healing quality and my mum always gave it to me when I was coming down with a cold. The spices and chilli were enough to drive the cold out of me. Usually served with plain boiled rice, this is a real pick-me-up.

2.5 litres vegetable stock
2 tbsp Ginger and Garlic Paste
  (see page 11)
1 tsp chilli powder
1 tbsp ground cumin
1 tbsp garam masala

1 tbsp hot paprika
2 tbsp freshly chopped coriander stalks
1 tbsp thyme leaves
1 tsp ground turmeric
4 medium tomatoes, roughly chopped
salt and freshly ground black pepper

1 Put half the vegetable stock and all the remaining ingredients into a blender or food processor and blitz until completely smooth.

2 Pour the soup into a large pan and place over a medium to high heat. Add the remaining vegetable stock. Bring to a simmer, reduce the heat and cook for 30 minutes. Serve hot with steamed basmati rice (see page 144).

DAHL AND AUBERGINE SOUP

SERVES 4-5

This is the ultimate comfort food. Perfect for rainy days, you can cook up big batches then chill it for up to 3 days to enjoy later in the week.

2 tbsp vegetable oil
1 shallot, finely chopped
2 garlic cloves, finely chopped
2.5cm piece of fresh root ginger,
  peeled and finely chopped
1 bird's eye chilli, finely chopped,
  plus extra to garnish
2 sprigs of thyme
250g brown lentils
2 plum tomatoes, chopped

1 litre vegetable stock
1 medium aubergine, chopped
  into 2.5cm cubes
warm wholemeal pitta bread,
  to serve

TO GARNISH
finely chopped red chilli
freshly chopped coriander
sliced spring onion

1 Heat the oil in a large pan over a medium heat and fry the shallot until translucent but not browned. Add the garlic and ginger and fry for 2 minutes, then add the chilli and thyme and cook for a couple of minutes, until the aromas are released from the thyme.

2 Add the lentils and stir to coat with the shallot mixture, then add the tomatoes and cook for 3 minutes. Pour over the vegetable stock and the same amount of water and bring to a simmer. Reduce the heat, cover and cook for 30 minutes. Add the aubergine and cook for 15–20 minutes until the lentils are soft but still have some bite.

3 Garnish with the chilli, coriander and spring onion and serve with the warm pitta bread.

GREEN PAPAYA SALAD SERVES 4

When the other *MasterChef* finalists and I flew out to Thailand, I remember John and Gregg saying that if you can master the art of Thai cuisine, you can conquer anything. The balance of flavours, from hot, sour, sweet and salty, can be tricky to get right. This is a classic example, a simple dish that performs a complete taste explosion on your tongue.

1 green papaya, peeled and seeded
2 large carrots, peeled

FOR THE DRESSING
1 garlic clove, crushed
3 tbsp freshly chopped coriander
   stalks, leaves reserved
1 bird's eye chilli, chopped

1 tbsp dried shrimp, soaked
   in hot water until soft and
   then drained (optional)
1 tbsp vegetable oil
juice of 3 limes
1 tbsp dark brown sugar
1 tbsp fish sauce
1 tbsp sweet chilli sauce

1 Using a mandolin, julienne the green papaya and carrot, or cut into thin matchsticks with a sharp knife.

2 To make the dressing, pound all of the ingredients together using a large pestle and mortar. Taste and adjust the seasoning if necessary – it should be sweet, salty and hot.

3 Place the papaya, carrot and reserved coriander leaves into a serving bowl. Pour over the dressing, mix to combine and serve.

FRESH CARROT SALAD SERVES 4-6

This originates from France and is a fresh and simple salad that you can prepare in advance and dress just before serving.

4 large carrots, peeled
2 banana shallots, finely sliced
handful of freshly chopped
   flat-leaf parsley, to garnish

FOR THE DRESSING
1½ tbsp white wine vinegar
3 tbsp rapeseed oil
salt and freshly ground black pepper

1 Using a mandolin, julienne the carrot, or cut into thin matchsticks with a sharp knife. Place into a large salad bowl and add the shallots.

2 To make the dressing, pour the white wine vinegar and rapeseed oil into a jam jar, add seasoning and shake thoroughly until completely emulsified. Pour over the carrots and shallots, sprinkle over the parsley and serve.

VARIATION

This dish can be transformed into a cucumber salad. You will need 2 white cucumbers, although if you can't find these just use regular cucumbers and peel them and remove the seeds. Serve garnished with a finely chopped green chilli and you have a Mauritian cucumber salad.

FENNEL AND MANGO SALAD

SERVES 3

I know this sounds like an odd combination, but it is a real burst of summer on a plate. The mangoes you tend to find in the supermarkets are bigger and milder in flavour and for this recipe will hold their shape better than Alphonso or Kesar mangoes found in Mauritius. The sweetness of the mango complements the aniseed of the fennel perfectly. This is a great companion to Spicy Soft-shell Crab (see page 64).

1 fennel bulb, trimmed
2 large semi-ripe mangoes (see above)
1 red chilli, roughly chopped
1½ tsp brown sugar
juice of 2 limes
1 tsp black mustard seeds, toasted
3 tbsp freshly chopped coriander
salt and freshly ground black pepper

1 Slice the fennel into thin strips, discarding the tough base. Place in a salad bowl.

2 Peel the skin from the mangoes and then cut the flesh into thin strips with a sharp knife. Add to the bowl with the fennel.

3 Add the remaining ingredients to the bowl, stir to combine and serve immediately.

RICE, NOODLES,
BREAD AND PASTA

Every country has its staple carbohydrates, whether it's potatoes in Ireland and the UK, pasta in Italy or rice and noodles in China. In Mauritius we get our carbs in a number of ways due to the many cultural and culinary influences. The Chinese brought noodles, the Europeans brought bread and the Indians gave us rice and unleavened breads such as roti and puri.

PERFECT STEAMED RICE SERVES 4

A lot of people have problems when cooking rice; well, fear not because this method is foolproof and fail-safe! My friend Serwah taught me this technique when we were at university. I remember her showing me and thinking, it'll never work... but to this day, it has never failed me. It uses the absorption method, whereby all the water you add to the rice gets absorbed and there is no need to drain it at the end. This way of cooking ensures that every grain is perfectly plump and not overcooked.

225g basmati rice   pinch of salt

1 First wash the rice. I like to wash it in the pan I will be cooking it in as this makes life easier! Pour the rice into a large pan and cover with cold water. Stir gently, swirling the rice around to remove some of the starchiness from the rice. Drain and return the rice to the pan.

2 Now add the cold water to the pan. It doesn't matter whether you are cooking more or less rice than the amount stated above – the point is that you measure the water by eye. Add enough cold water to cover the rice by approximately 2.5 cm. I like to use my index finger as a marker – the water sitting on top of the rice should come up to the first crease on your finger. Add a pinch of salt, cover the pan with foil and then put the lid on top so that the pan is sealed. This will ensure that the rice is completely steamed.

3 Cook over a medium to high heat for 6–7 minutes. Reduce the heat and simmer for a further 5 minutes. Remove from the heat and leave with the lid on for a further 10 minutes – the rice will continue to steam in this time. Do not peek or open the foil at all as the steam will escape. After the 10 minutes you will have perfectly cooked steamed rice.

FRIED RICE SERVES 8

This is a Sino-Mauritian dish which is very much a party dish in our house, usually reserved for big family gatherings and birthdays as we normally make it in huge quantities. My mum gets me to prepare all the vegetables as her sous-chef – she still doesn't trust me to put the dish together, which is the best part! I get so much satisfaction from making this dish now, but for some strange reason, it just never tastes as good as Mum's. I'm sure she is adding ingredients that she hasn't told me about... This version, nonetheless, still tastes great.

The best tip I can give you is to make sure all the vegetables are chopped to the same size so that they cook evenly.

2 tbsp vegetable oil
1 large Spanish onion, thinly sliced
3 garlic cloves, finely chopped
½ white cabbage, finely shredded
2 carrots, peeled and chopped
  into matchsticks
1 x 200g tin sweetcorn, drained

5 tbsp light soy sauce
3 tbsp oyster sauce
2 tbsp sesame oil
500g steamed basmati rice
  (see page 144)
3 tbsp finely chopped garlic chives
Garlic Water (see page 170), to serve

1 Heat the vegetable oil in a large wok and fry the onions and garlic until slightly softened, about 3 minutes. Add the cabbage, carrots and sweetcorn and stir-fry for around 3–4 minutes, making sure that you are constantly moving the vegetables around the wok to cook them evenly and to make sure that they don't stick to the bottom of the wok and burn.

2 Add the soy sauce, oyster sauce and sesame oil and cook for a further 3–4 minutes, then add the cooked rice and mix in thoroughly, making sure that all the grains are coated in the mixture.

3 Once the rice is reheated and evenly coated, sprinkle in the chopped garlic chives and remove from the heat. This dish is usually served with Garlic Water – sprinkle about 2 tablespoons over each serving.

PORK BOL RENVERSE SERVES 4

This popular dish would be on the menu of any good Sino-Mauritian restaurant. It is such a simple recipe but at the same time is great for dinner parties as it has a sense of drama and anticipation. *Bol renversé* means 'upside-down bowl' and at the last moment you lift up the bowl from the plate to reveal the deliciously hot and fragrant rice and stir-fried meat, topped off with a perfectly runny fried egg.

1 tbsp cornflour
vegetable oil for frying
1 medium onion, finely diced
2 garlic cloves, finely chopped
200g pork tenderloin fillet,
    cut into thin strips
2 medium carrots, peeled and
    cut into matchsticks
2 baby pak choy, leaves finely sliced

5–6 shiitake mushrooms,
    sliced lengthways
3 tbsp light soy sauce
1–2 tbsp oyster sauce
1 tsp rice wine vinegar
1 tsp white pepper
4 eggs
400g steamed basmati rice
    (see page 144)

1 In a small bowl mix together the cornflour and 250ml of cold water. Make sure the cornflour has completely dissolved and that there are no lumps.

2 Heat a little vegetable oil in a wok or large frying pan and add the onion. Allow to soften slightly, then add the garlic and cook for about 1–2 minutes, taking care not to burn it. Add the pork and seal on all sides – this should take about 2 minutes – then add the carrots, pak choy and mushrooms and cook for 2 minutes. Add the soy sauce, oyster sauce, rice wine vinegar and white pepper, then add the cornflour with water and allow to cook for approximately 4–5 minutes until all the vegetables are cooked through.

3 Heat a little vegetable oil in a separate frying pan and fry the eggs, one at a time. Cook them sunny-side up, making sure you baste the top of the egg with hot oil so that it is sealed on top – this should take about 1–2 minutes.

4 To serve, divide the pork and vegetable mixture between 4 cereal bowls. Top with the steamed rice and press down firmly. Turn out on to a plate – you should have a perfect round shape. Place a fried egg on top and, if you like, carefully put the bowl back before serving so you can reveal the egg at the table.

VEGETABLE PILAU SERVES 8

2 tbsp vegetable oil
4 spring onions, chopped
1 courgette, chopped into matchsticks
4 cardamom pods, crushed
1 cinnamon stick, snapped in half
1 tsp cayenne pepper

500g white basmati rice
100g frozen petits pois
800–900ml vegetable stock
50g flaked almonds
2 tbsp freshly chopped flat-leaf parsley
salt and freshly ground black pepper

1 Heat the oil in a large, heavy-based pan with a tight-fitting lid and add the spring onions, courgette, cardamom pods, cinnamon, cayenne pepper and salt and pepper. Cook for about 2 minutes and then add the rice. Stir so that each grain of rice is coated in the oil and spices.

2 Add the petits pois and enough vegetable stock to cover the rice with 2.5cm of liquid. Cover with a piece of foil and then the lid. Cook over a medium heat for 12 minutes. Remove from the heat but leave the lid on for a further 10 minutes so that the rice continues to cook from the heat in the pan.

3 In a separate dry frying pan, toast the almonds until they just start to colour and give off their aroma. Once the rice has rested for 10 minutes, fork through the almonds and chopped parsley, being careful not to break up the rice grains. Serve immediately.

CUMIN AND SAFFRON RICE SERVES 4

This is a lovely accompaniment to the *Rougaille Poisson Salé* (see page 59).

1 tsp vegetable oil
1 tbsp cumin seeds
200g basmati rice

pinch of saffron strands
  (see Note)
½ tsp salt

1 Heat the vegetable oil in a large pan with a tight-fitting lid and add the cumin seeds. Toast them for a couple of minutes, until you can smell the cumin aroma being released.

2 Add the rice, saffron and salt and then add enough cold water to cover the rice by approximately 2.5cm. Cover the top of the pan with foil and then place a lid completely over the top so that the pan is sealed. Cook over a medium heat for 15 minutes. Don't be tempted to peep, not even once. You want to trap the steam as this is what makes the rice so deliciously fluffy.

NOTE
If you don't have saffron you can substitute it with 1 tablespoon of ground turmeric.

BRIANI CELEBRATION RICE SERVES 6

This is a regular feature at every wedding, birthday or christening. Traditionally it is layered more slowly but my version means you can make celebration rice quickly, without sacrificing any of the delicious flavours.

vegetable oil for deep-frying
1 white onion, finely sliced
4 garlic cloves, finely sliced
2 large potatoes, peeled and chopped
  into 2cm cubes
1 tbsp ground cumin
1 tbsp ground coriander
1 tbsp garam masala
10 whole green cardamom pods,
  crushed
1 tsp cumin seeds, toasted (see page 10)

300g white basmati rice
pinch of salt
2 tbsp freshly chopped coriander
2 tbsp freshly chopped mint
pinch of saffron strands
20g unsalted butter

TO GARNISH
3 semi-soft-boiled eggs, peeled
  and quartered
2 tbsp freshly chopped coriander

1 Heat enough oil for deep-frying in a deep-sided, heavy-based pan until a cube of day-old bread dropped into it sizzles and turns golden brown in 30 seconds. Alternatively heat a deep-fat fryer to 180°C.

2 Lower the onion and garlic slices into the hot oil and deep-fry until golden-brown. Remove with a slotted spoon and drain on kitchen paper.

3 Add the potatoes and deep-fry for around 4–5 minutes until the potatoes are golden on the outside and cooked all the way through. Remove and drain on kitchen paper.

4 Put the spices, rice, fried garlic, onions, potatoes, salt, coriander and mint in a separate large pan with a tight-fitting lid and mix together. Sprinkle over the saffron strands (don't mix in as you don't want a uniform colour) and dot with the butter. Add enough water to cover the rice with 2.5cm of liquid. Cover with a piece of foil and then the lid and cook over a medium heat for 15–20 minutes.

5 Remove the rice from the heat and leave to steam with the lid on – you need the residual heat to steam the rice for another 15 minutes.

6 Spoon on to a large platter and garnish with the eggs and coriander.

WILD RICE WITH BLACK LENTILS

SERVES 4-6

Otherwise known as urid beans, these black lentils are similar to mung beans, but have a sweeter taste and retain their shape better than other lentils and pulses. Interestingly, when you buy white lentils they are actually black lentils with their skins removed. I love this lentil as it is high in fibre and transforms this dish into something quite delicious. I usually serve this rice alongside a roasted fish dish.

100g black lentils (urid beans)
300g wild rice

2 tbsp freshly chopped coriander
and flat-leaf parsley
salt and freshly ground black pepper

1 Bring a large pan of water to the boil and cook the black lentils for 25 minutes, until just tender. Drain and rinse with fresh cold water and leave to one side.

2 Put the wild rice, cooked black lentils and salt and pepper into the same pan and add enough water to cover the rice and lentils with 2.5cm of liquid. Cover with a piece of foil and then a lid and cook over a medium to low heat for 30 minutes.

3 Remove from the heat but leave the lid on for an additional 10 minutes after cooking to allow the rice and lentils to steam. Remove the lid from the pan and fork through the chopped parsley and coriander. Serve hot.

EGG-FRIED RICE SERVES 4-6

There are so many different versions of this recipe but this is the recipe my mum has used for years. It is always perfect and is a great way to use up day-old rice.

1 tbsp vegetable oil
1 garlic clove, finely chopped
4 spring onions, finely chopped
4 large eggs, lightly beaten

75g frozen petits pois, defrosted
300g cooked long-grain rice
3 tbsp light soy sauce
1 tbsp sesame oil

1 Heat the vegetable oil in a large wok over a high heat and add the chopped garlic and spring onions. Stir-fry for 2 minutes, then add the beaten egg and cook for 1 minute, stirring quickly so that the egg cooks through. When the egg is semi-set add the petit pois, rice, soy sauce and sesame oil and stir-fry for 3 minutes until everything is evenly cooked and the rice is piping hot.

2 This rice perfectly complements the Chinese-style Beef with Green Peppers (see page 99).

MIN FRIRE SERVES 6

The best *min frire* (fried noodles) I ever had was in Chinatown in Mauritius. It is really simple to prepare and is usually served with Garlic Water (see page 170).

8 bundles dried egg noodles
1 tbsp sesame oil
2 tbsp vegetable oil
1 garlic clove, finely chopped
2cm piece of fresh root ginger, peeled and grated

½ white cabbage, finely chopped
2 carrots, peeled and chopped into matchsticks
2 tbsp dark soy sauce
1 tbsp oyster sauce
2 tbsp finely chopped garlic chives

1 Cook the dried noodles in boiling water according to the packet instructions, until just cooked or al dente. Drain and toss through with the sesame oil to prevent the noodles from sticking. Set aside.

2 Heat the vegetable oil in a wok, add the garlic and ginger and fry for 1 minute until fragrant. Add the cabbage and carrots and cook for 4–5 minutes, stirring constantly to prevent anything from burning at the bottom of the wok.

3 Add the cooked noodles, soy sauce and oyster sauce and stir-fry for another 2 minutes, making sure all the noodles are mixed with the vegetables and have taken on the colour from the soy sauce. Remove from the heat, toss through the garlic chives and serve immediately.

QUINOA PILAU

SERVES 4-6

1 tbsp olive oil
2 garlic cloves, finely chopped
1 tsp yellow mustard seeds
½ tsp ground black pepper
1 tsp ground turmeric
1 tsp ground coriander
1 tsp garam masala

½ tsp ground cumin
225g quinoa
½ tsp salt
1 x 400g tin kidney beans, drained
1 tbsp freshly chopped mint
1 tbsp freshly chopped coriander

1 Heat the olive oil in a heavy-based pan with a tight-fitting lid over a medium to low heat. Add the garlic and sauté for 1 minute, then add the mustard seeds, black pepper, turmeric, coriander, garam masala and cumin and sauté for 2 minutes, until the aromas of the spices hit your nose.

2 Increase the heat slightly, add the quinoa and toss through to make sure every grain is coated in the spices and seasoning. Add the salt and enough water to cover the quinoa with 2.5cm of liquid. Cover with a piece of foil and then the lid. Reduce the heat and cook for approximately 30 minutes.

3 Add the kidney beans and stir through for a few minutes to warm through. Scatter with the fresh mint and coriander and serve warm.

KEDGEREE SERVES 3-4

This is the perfect brunch recipe; it's also great the morning after the night before. Delicately spiced and with a protein boost from both the eggs and the mackerel, it's ideal hangover food. You can substitute the mackerel for tofu for a vegetarian version of this recipe.

1 tbsp olive oil
1 banana shallot, finely diced
2 garlic cloves, finely chopped
1 medium green chilli, finely chopped
1 tsp ground turmeric
1 tsp black mustard seeds
2 tsp cumin seeds, toasted (see page 10)
1 tsp smoked paprika
½ tsp salt
½ tsp pepper

150g white basmati rice
320ml water
100g smoked mackerel fillets, skinned

TO GARNISH
2 spring onions, roughly chopped
2 hard-boiled eggs, quartered
1 tbsp chopped fresh parsley
1 lime, cut into wedges

1 Heat the olive oil in a skillet or large frying pan with a tight-fitting lid and cook the shallot, garlic and chilli for around 3–4 minutes, until softened. Add all the spices along with the salt and pepper and fry for 2 more minutes.

2 Add the basmati rice and water and cover with a piece of foil and then the lid. Reduce the heat and simmer for approximately 12 minutes.

3 Once the rice is cooked, flake in the smoked mackerel and stir through gently to allow the fish to warm through. Scatter over the chopped spring onions, eggs and parsley and serve with the lime wedges.

MACARONI AND CHICKEN SERVES 6

Mum used to make this for us when we were little and it was a firm favourite in our house. She would prepare it when she knew she would be working late and leave it on the stove for us to tuck into after school. I'm sure my Italian relatives will say this recipe is blasphemous to the 'sacred' pasta, but sometimes it's worth going against tradition as this really is comfort food at its best.

1 tbsp olive oil
2 banana shallots, finely chopped
2 garlic cloves, finely chopped
1 green chilli, finely chopped
4 sprigs of thyme
4 boneless chicken thighs,
   cut into 3cm pieces

250g macaroni
4 fresh tomatoes, preferably
   on the vine, chopped
½ tsp tomato purée
salt and freshly ground black pepper

1 Heat the olive oil in a large, heavy-based pan over a medium heat, add the shallots and cook until they are translucent. Add the garlic and chilli and cook for another 2 minutes, then add the thyme sprigs and chicken pieces. Seal the chicken until you get a golden colour on all sides, this usually takes around 5 minutes.

2 Meanwhile, cook the macaroni in a large pan of boiling salted water according to the packet instructions. Make sure the pasta is only cooked al dente as it will be cooked again in the chicken mixture.

3 Add the chopped tomatoes and tomato purée to the chicken and cook for around 5 minutes, until the tomatoes are completely cooked through and most of the liquid has evaporated. At this point, add about 100ml of water and salt and pepper and cook for a further 10 minutes.

4 Drain the pasta, add to the chicken mixture and stir through. Cook for a further 3 minutes. Serve immediately.

ROTI MAKES 10

This simple unleavened bread is made from just a handful of ingredients. The result is a deliciously soft and pliable bread which is so versatile and can be eaten alongside most Mauritian dishes. I love to eat these with Butter Bean Curry (see page 127) and *Satchini Pomme d'Amour* (see page 166), making a seriously wonderful meal using pretty much all store-cupboard ingredients.

300g plain white flour
4–5 tbsp vegetable oil, plus
   extra for frying

1 tbsp salt
150ml hot water, or enough
   to make a soft dough

1 Combine all the ingredients in a large mixing bowl and mix together to form a soft dough (you may need more or less water). Place in a pre-oiled bowl, cover with a damp cloth and allow to rest for 30 minutes.

2 Divide the dough into approximately 10 pieces and roll each one into a pancake shape. Brush a flat pancake pan with vegetable oil and cook the roti one at a time over a high heat. Cook them on both sides until they have patches of colour and are puffed up, this usually takes about 1–2 minutes. (Pictured on page 161.)

REDDIT
ROTI
CHAUD

DAL PURI MAKES 10

Dal puri is classic Mauritian street food. For me, it sums up the Mauritian food experience, and is the only dish that I *have* to have when visiting Mauritius, otherwise I feel like my trip is incomplete. It usually comes wrapped in paper or foil and if you're anything like me you will end up spilling it down your clothes when you eat it. It is totally worth it.

100g yellow split peas, soaked in water overnight with 1 tsp ground turmeric
700ml water
2 tsp ground turmeric

250g plain flour
3 tbsp vegetable oil, plus extra for frying
pinch of salt

1 Drain the yellow split peas and place in a large pan with the water and ground turmeric; bring to the boil. Cook until the peas just start to break up, about 25 minutes. Drain the peas, reserving the cooking liquid, and place the peas in a food processor or blender. Blitz until you get a very fine paste.

2 Put the flour, oil, salt and approximately 150ml of the reserved cooking water into a large bowl and mix together. Knead until you have a pliable dough (you may need to add more water) and then leave to rest for around 20–30 minutes in a pre-oiled bowl covered with a damp cloth.

3 Once the dough has rested, pull off a piece of dough the size of a small plum and roll into a ball using the palm of your hand. Push a small indentation into the middle of the ball and add a teaspoon of the yellow split pea paste, cover over and carefully form back into a ball. Using a rolling pin, roll out the ball into a circle about 15–20cm in diameter.

4 Heat a skillet or large frying pan to smoking and then use a pastry brush to brush the base of the pan with vegetable oil. Place the rolled-out dough straight on to the pan and allow to puff up and reveal lots of air pockets – this will take anywhere between 30 seconds and 1 minute. Flip the bread over and repeat on the other side. Continue until all the bread is cooked.

PURI MAKES 12

Puri bread is usually served with vegetables and pickles and is golden, puffy and very moreish! These deep-fried breads originated in India.

300g wholemeal flour, plus
   extra for dusting
1 tsp salt
1 tbsp cumin seeds
2 tbsp vegetable oil, plus extra
   for deep-frying

50ml full-fat milk
50ml hot water, or enough
   to create a soft dough

1 Put the flour, salt and cumin seeds in a large mixing bowl and make a well in the centre. Add the vegetable oil, milk and hot water, a little at a time, and mix into the flour to create a soft and pliable dough. Knead for a few minutes. Place in an oiled bowl, cover with a damp cloth and leave to rest for about 30 minutes.

2 Divide the dough into about 12 golf ball-sized portions and roll each one into balls using the palms of your hands. Lightly flour a work surface and roll each ball into a circle about 10–12 cm wide and about 0.5cm thick.

3 Heat enough vegetable oil for deep-frying in a large, heavy-based pan until a cube of day-old bread dropped into it sizzles and turns golden brown in 30 seconds. Alternatively heat a deep-fat fryer to 180°C. Deep-fry the puri for 1 minute on each side until golden brown and completely puffed up. Drain on kitchen paper to remove any excess oil and serve immediately.

ACCOMPANIMENTS

In Mauritius almost every dish and every meal is accompanied by a range of condiments, salsas, sauces and pickles; a Mauritian meal is not complete without them. Mauritian pickles are made with a range of fruit and vegetables and can be a great way to make use of an abundance of a certain fruit. A typical pickle, or 'achard', will contain vegetable oil, mustard seeds, black pepper, turmeric, chilli and garlic. You will find some classic condiments from the island here, as well as a few 'Shelina' additions...

It's difficult to give exact yield quantities but all these recipes make enough to serve 4–6 people as a side dish to a main meal or as an accompaniment to *gajaks*.

CORIANDER AND MINT CHUTNEY

This is such a simple chutney and is perfect with *Gâteaux Piments with Crab* (see page 22).

5 tbsp freshly chopped coriander
2 tbsp freshly chopped mint
2 tbsp vegetable oil

2 ripe tomatoes
1 garlic clove
salt to taste

1 Place all the ingredients in a food processor or use a hand blender to blitz until fully combined.

2 This is best prepared and served fresh, but will last up to a day in an airtight container in the fridge.

SATCHINI POMME D'AMOUR

A delicious tomato chutney with heat from the chilli which is perfect with fish and seafood.

4 ripe tomatoes
1 garlic clove
3 tbsp freshly chopped coriander stalk

1–2 tbsp vegetable oil
1 red bird's eye chilli
salt to taste

1 Place all ingredients in a food processor or blender and blitz until completely smooth. Serve immediately with any number of *gajaks* or as an accompaniment to a main meal.

SATCHINI COCO

A fresh and zingy coconut chutney.

1 brown coconut, flesh finely grated	squeeze of lime juice
1 garlic clove	100ml coconut milk
1 tbsp freshly chopped coriander	3 green chillies
1 tbsp tamarind paste	salt to taste

1 Place the grated coconut into a hot skillet or frying pan and toast until lightly brown, about 2–3 minutes. This will help release the natural oils.

2 Place the toasted coconut in a food processor or blender with all the remaining ingredients and blitz until completely combined. The chutney will last for up to 5 days in the fridge in an airtight container.

NOTE

The traditional way of making this would be to use a 'roche cari', which is two pieces of stone. The ingredients are placed on one flat stone, and another stone is used on top, a bit like a rolling pin, and rolled back and forth over the ingredients. Slowly but surely the ingredients would turn into a fine paste… I don't know about you, but I'm quite glad to own a food processor!

GARLIC WATER

This is a typically Mauritian condiment, most often used with *Min Frire* (see page 154) or *Fried Rice* (see page 145), although I also like to use it with fish and seafood dishes. It is simply a flavoured water that is sprinkled over a hot dish just before serving, adding a wonderful depth of flavour.

1 tbsp unrefined golden caster sugar
500ml hot water
100ml white wine vinegar

1 garlic clove, finely chopped
3 tbsp finely chopped garlic chives
1 tsp salt, or to taste

1 Dissolve the sugar in about half the hot water, stirring until it has completely dissolved. Add all the remaining ingredients and leave to steep for about 1 hour.

2 Garlic water can be stored in an airtight container in the fridge for up to 1 week.

MANGO AND APPLE VINEGAR

This is a great to have to hand in the fridge. I love sprinkling it over plain grilled fish or seafood and it's great for spritzing up an otherwise boring green salad.

100ml mango juice
100ml apple juice
25ml cider vinegar

juice of 1 lime
salt and freshly ground black pepper

1 Place all the ingredients in a squeezy bottle or a sterilised glass jar and give it a good shake to combine all the flavours. Place in the fridge and keep for up to 10 days.

SPICY REMOULADE

300ml good-quality mayonnaise
1 garlic clove
1 tsp cayenne pepper
1 red chilli, seeded and finely chopped

2 tbsp freshly chopped coriander stalks
2 tbsp Dijon mustard
salt and freshly ground black pepper

1 Place all the ingredients in a bowl and mix until completely combined.

2 Taste and adjust the seasoning. Keep for up to 2 days in the fridge.

THAI DIPPING SAUCE

This dipping sauce goes perfectly with the Tamarind Red Bream (see page 31).

3 tbsp light soy sauce
2 tbsp rice wine vinegar
juice of 1 lime

3 tbsp fish sauce
2 tbsp muscovado sugar

1 Place all the ingredients in a bowl and mix thoroughly.

2 You can double or even triple the quantities given here to make a big batch of this. It will last for up to a month in the fridge in a sterile container.

MAZAVAROO

This chilli and prawn paste is ferociously hot. Call me weird, but I actually eat this spread on toast, although normal people would generally have this as an accompaniment to a curry or rice dish. It works well with quite a few of the *gajaks* in this book, particularly the Chicken and Pork Steamed Dumplings (see page 28).

300g dried shrimp, soaked
  in hot water for 15 minutes
10 red bird's eye chillies
3 banana shallots, chopped

2 garlic cloves
6 tbsp white wine vinegar
8 tbsp vegetable oil
salt

1 Drain the soaked shrimp and dry on kitchen paper. Place in a food processor or blender along with all the other ingredients, excluding the vegetable oil. Blitz until you have a smooth, thick paste.

2 Heat about half the oil in a large pan and add the paste. Cook for 2–3 minutes until the moisture comes out of the paste. Once cooked, place in a small sterile jar and allow to cool. Top up with the remaining oil before placing in the fridge. This should last about 3 weeks in the fridge.

MANGO KUTCHA

Kutcha is a Hindi word which means 'smashed up'. This is traditionally made on a stone rolling board ('roche cari') where the mango is crushed into a paste. I've made life easier here by grating the mango.

2 tbsp vegetable oil, plus extra for
   topping
1 tbsp ground turmeric
2 red chillies, finely chopped
1 tbsp mustard seeds

1 garlic clove, finely chopped
30–40ml white wine vinegar
2–3 unripe green mangoes,
   peeled and grated
1 tsp salt, or to taste

1 Heat the vegetable oil in a pan and add the turmeric, chillies, mustard seeds and garlic and cook for about 1 minute over a medium heat.

2 Add the vinegar and then the mangoes and salt and cook for another 2–3 minutes.

3 Allow to cool down before placing in an airtight container, cover the top with oil and then seal the container. Store in the fridge for up to 2 weeks.

VARIATION
You can make a banana pickle by substituting the mangoes for 2–3 grated unripe green bananas.

SIMPLE SPICY SALAD DRESSING

This dressing is lovely on a fresh green salad, as well as drizzled over any roasted meat or grilled fish/seafood, it's incredibly versatile and will keep in the fridge for up to a week.

2 tsp cumin seeds, toasted
  (see page 10)
200ml vegetable oil
2 red chillies, finely chopped

juice of 2–3 limes
2 tbsp freshly snipped garlic chives
2 tbsp freshly chopped coriander stalk
salt and freshly ground black pepper

1 Grind the toasted cumin seeds to a powder using a pestle and mortar.

2 Tip into a bowl and add all the other ingredients. Whisk until completely combined.

3 Place in a sterile jar and use whenever you need. It will keep for up to 5 days in the fridge.

SWEET DELIGHTS
AND MANGO LOVE

I earned a bit of a reputation on *MasterChef* for being the 'Mango Queen' and rightly so! I think I used mango in pretty much every one of my dishes, to the extent that some people thought that I was a secret mango dealer. I remember the first time I made my mango trifle on the show; Gregg Wallace said it was possibly the best dessert he'd ever eaten. I have to thank Gregg for saying that as his comments really fuelled me to work harder in the competition. He also said I should have been a pastry chef; strangely enough, I don't actually have a sweet tooth.

However, since the show I've discovered a love of the art of pastry and find it really relaxing. I love to spend my weekends mulling over dessert recipes or playing with pastry and bread. There is something so satisfying about it and so luxurious; a delicious dessert can turn a good dinner into a great dinner.

There are quite a few gluten-free desserts in this chapter which I hope you will enjoy making and, of course, a smattering of mango-inspired dishes which I hope will ignite in you a love affair with my favourite fruit!

SPICED TEA RUM BABAS MAKES 4

Apparently babas originated in Poland and then evolved into different styles across Europe. This version is not only heady with spiced rum, but is infused with chai tea, giving it a real depth of character. Utterly divine and a real show-off dessert for special occasions.

FOR THE BABA
75g plain flour
10g fast-action dried yeast
25g milk powder
15g unrefined golden caster sugar
zest of 1 lemon
2 egg yolks
55ml warm milk
40g unsalted butter

FOR THE SPICED TEA SYRUP
200g unrefined light muscovado sugar
200g unrefined golden caster sugar
300ml water
2 tbsp masala chai tea
5 whole star anise
10 cardamom pods
1 cinnamon sticks
small pinch of salt
2 tsp rosewater
zest of 1 orange
70ml spiced Mauritian rum

1 To make the baba, mix together the flour, dried yeast, milk powder, sugar and lemon zest in one bowl. In a separate bowl, mix the egg yolks with the warm milk and butter and then slowly stir this into the dry mixture. Place in an oiled bowl, cover with a damp cloth and leave for 30 minutes to allow it to rise.

2 The dough should now resemble a thick batter. Grease four holes in a large, deep muffin tray then divide the mixture between them. Allow to rest for another 30 minutes. Preheat oven to 180°C/gas 4.

3 When the babas have risen again, place the tin in the oven and cook for 15 minutes until golden brown and nicely risen.

4 To make the syrup, place all the ingredients in a pan over a low heat. Simmer for about 5 minutes until the sugar has dissolved and the tea has infused into the mixture. Tip the syrup into a shallow dish and allow to cool. Once the babas are cooked, turn them out of the the tin, drench them in the spiced sugar syrup and leave to soak for 30 minutes before serving.

CHAI TIRAMISU SERVES 6-8

Masala chai is a traditional Indian beverage made by brewing tea with a mixture of aromatic spices. It is available in Asian grocers as well as in many large supermarkets.

2 tbsp masala chai tea
250ml boiling water
75ml spiced Mauritian rum
5 egg yolks
120g unrefined golden caster sugar

1 vanilla pod, seeds scraped (see page 11)
750g mascarpone
200g savoiardi sponge fingers
100g dark cocoa powder
100g pistachios, crushed

1 Brew the chai tea in the boiling water and allow to steep for around 5 minutes, then strain. Add the spiced rum and then pour into a shallow dish and set aside.

2 Using a hand-held mixer, whisk the egg yolks with the sugar and the vanilla seeds for about 10 minutes. The mixture needs to have at least tripled in size and should be a very pale yellow and really aerated. Slowly mix in the mascarpone.

3 To assemble the tiramisu dip each sponge finger in the chai and rum mixture and lay into a 23 x 33cm rectangular serving dish; continue until you have covered the base. Now evenly spread over about one-third of the mascarpone mixture and then dust over some cocoa powder and sprinkle with crushed pistachios. Continue layering until you have created about two or three layers. Finish with a layer of cocoa powder and crushed pistachios.

4 Place in the fridge and chill for a few hours before serving.

GINGER AND LIME PIE SERVES 6-8

225g ginger biscuits
80g unsalted butter, melted
30g unrefined molasses sugar, plus
  extra for decorating

250ml double cream
1 x 400g tin condensed milk
juice and zest of 5–6 limes

1 Put the ginger biscuits into a large plastic bag (a sandwich bag is ideal) and bash vigorously with a rolling pin until you have a bag of crumbs.

2 Put the butter and sugar in a pan and heat until the butter has melted and the sugar completely dissolved. Add the crumbs to the pan and stir until all the crumbs are coated in the butter. Tip the crumb mixture into a 23cm pie dish or cake tin and press down firmly to create the base of the pie – you need to make sure there are no air pockets. Place in the fridge to chill for about 20 minutes.

3 Put the double cream, condensed milk, lime juice and zest (reserve a little of the lime zest for decoration) into a large bowl and use an electric whisk to whisk until the mixture is stiff. Spoon this mixture on top of the biscuit base and then return to the fridge to chill for about 4 hours.

4 Just before serving, scatter with the reserved lime zest and a little molasses sugar.

LYCHEE PANNA COTTA SERVES 6

FOR THE PANNA COTTA
400ml double cream
75g unrefined golden caster sugar
100ml lychee purée (see Notes)
3 leaves gelatine, soaked in cold
    water to soften (see Notes)

FOR THE JELLY
220ml passion fruit juice (see Notes)
50g unrefined golden caster sugar
2 leaves gelatine, soaked in
    cold water to soften

TO DECORATE
6 fresh lychees, peeled and stoned
    (optional)
3 passion fruit, halved and pulp sieved

1 Start by making the panna cotta. Place the cream, sugar and lychee purée in a pan and heat until the sugar has dissolved, then remove from the heat. Squeeze the water from the soaked gelatine leaves, add to the pan and whisk until the gelatine has completely dissolved. Pour the mixture through a fine sieve and into a jug. Pour the mixture into six glasses and chill in the fridge for at least 1½ hours to set.

2 Make the jelly. Heat the passion fruit juice and sugar together in a pan until the sugar has dissolved, then remove from the heat. Squeeze the excess water from the gelatine sheets and add to the pan. Whisk until the gelatine has dissolved and then strain through a fine sieve so that there are no lumps in the jelly. Divide this mixture equally between the glasses.

3 To decorate, place a lychee on top of each glass and then drizzle over some fresh passion fruit flesh (sieve if you prefer it without the crunch of the seeds). Serve immediately.

NOTES

Lychee purée is available from online suppliers but you can make your own by peeling and stoning lychees and blitzing.

For a vegetarian alternative to gelatine, use 1 tablespoon of agar agar powder.

Passion fruit juice can be bought in most large supermarkets.

RASGULLA MAKES 10

These deliciously sweet dumplings are usually eaten on special occasions, weddings and big family gatherings and I remember my mum frying up huge batches when I was a child. The house would be filled with the smell of sweetened milk and cardamom, such a comforting memory.

Rasgulla are traditionally made using milk curd. I've simplified this recipe by using powdered milk.

FOR THE SUGAR SYRUP
1 cinnamon stick, broken in half
1 star anise
4–5 green cardamom pods, crushed
200g unrefined golden caster sugar
200ml water

FOR THE RASGULLA
125g powdered milk
20g self-raising flour
1 tbsp vegetable oil
1 egg, beaten
vegetable oil for frying
vanilla ice cream, to serve

1 To prepare the sugar syrup, place all the ingredients into a pan and heat gently for about 5 minutes until the sugar has dissolved. Remove the whole spices from the syrup and set aside to cool.

2 Mix the powdered milk and self-raising flour in a bowl until well combined then add the oil and egg. Mix until you have a soft dough. Take small pieces of the dough and roll into small balls, about the size of a lychee, using the palms of your hands.

3 Heat a little vegetable oil in a large heavy-based pan and fry the rasgulla over a medium heat for about 8–10 minutes, until golden brown and evenly cooked on all sides. Remove from the pan, drain on kitchen paper and place straight into the sugar syrup. Leave the rasgulla to steep in the syrup for at least 1 hour, turning occasionally.

4 Serve with good vanilla ice cream – delicious!

POLENTA PUDDING SERVES 6-8

Now, there are two ways to eat this pudding. You can eat it hot, as my siblings and I used to for breakfast, or you can let it chill in the fridge and have it as an after-school snack. My mum used to whip this up if she knew family were popping over as it's quite easy to put together and just needs a few hours to set in the fridge. Most Mauritians will know and love this recipe.

200ml cold water
400ml full-fat milk
200ml single cream
75g unrefined golden caster sugar
1 vanilla pod, seeds scraped
  (see page 11)
1 tbsp coconut oil (use rapeseed oil
  if you can't get hold of coconut oil)

250g polenta (cornmeal)
50g desiccated coconut
50g sultanas
vegetable oil for greasing

TO DECORATE
2 tbsp desiccated coconut
1 tbsp unrefined icing sugar

1 Put the water, milk, cream, sugar, vanilla seeds, coconut oil and polenta into a large, heavy-based pan and place over a low heat until the mixture comes to a gentle simmer.

2 Add the desiccated coconut and sultanas to the pan and cook for about 5 minutes, stirring often to make sure the bottom of the pan doesn't burn. Once all the liquid has evaporated from the mixture, tip into a lightly oiled dish and allow to cool. Chill in the fridge for 2 hours. Sprinkle over the coconut and icing sugar just before serving. Serve with fresh fruit.

RICE VERMICELLI CAKE SERVES 6-8

I used to absolutely love this dessert when I was growing up. Unsurprisingly, when I mentioned it to my Italian husband he was completely and utterly confused, as for him, vermicelli is something you eat in a savoury dish. The concept is not far off that of a traditional rice pudding, but using rice vermicelli or 'glass noodles' instead. This deliciously sweet and fragrant dessert is also completely gluten-free.

1 tbsp unsalted butter, plus extra
   for greasing
30g flaked almonds
1 vanilla pod, seeds scraped (see page 11)
30g sultanas

500ml full-fat milk
200ml water
80g unrefined golden caster sugar
1 tsp mixed spice
150g rice vermicelli

1 In a large, heavy-based pan, melt the butter over a medium heat then add the almonds and cook for about 2–3 minutes.

2 Add the vanilla seeds to the pan along with the sultanas, milk, water, sugar and mixed spice and allow to come to a simmer. At this point, add the vermicelli and cook for about 3–5 minutes, until the vermicelli is cooked through and starts to soak up the water and milk in the pan. Remove from the heat and place into a lightly buttered dish (I prefer a rectangular dish, but this is just my preference). Allow to cool and then refrigerate for 2 hours before serving.

TIP
Once you've scraped out the seeds from the vanilla pod, do not throw the pod away. Add it to a jar of sugar to make vanilla sugar, or add to a bottle of dark rum to add vanilla tones to it.

BAKED RICOTTA CAKE WITH PINEAPPLE COULIS SERVES 4

I love finding new recipes that are gluten-free as I have quite a few friends who have gluten allergies. This really doesn't feel like a 'free from' dessert – it's so delicious that everyone will love it.

FOR THE CAKES
2 egg whites
75g unrefined golden caster sugar
200g ricotta
15g ground almonds
20ml single cream
vegetable oil for greasing

FOR THE PINEAPPLE COULIS
½ fresh pineapple, peeled, cored and cut into chunks
100g unrefined golden caster sugar
juice of ½ lime

1 Place all the ingredients for the coulis into a food processor and blitz until completely smooth. Chill in the fridge until ready to serve.

2 Preheat the oven to 160°C/gas 2½. In a bowl, mix together the egg whites, sugar, ricotta, ground almonds and cream until smooth and well combined.

3 Divide the mixture equally between four lightly oiled ramekins and then place them into a roasting tray. Create a bain marie by pouring boiling water into the tray to reach halfway up the sides of the ramekins. Bake the ricotta mixture in the oven for 20 minutes until the mixture is set with a slight 'wobble'.

4 Allow to cool before serving with the pineapple coulis.

MANGO CREME BRULEE SERVES 6

A tropical twist on one of my favourite desserts. I absolutely love mangoes (if you hadn't realised already) and this adds a wonderful aromatic flavour to a classic and elegant dessert. You can make these well in advance as they keep in the fridge for up to 2 days.

500ml double cream
1 vanilla pod
6 cardamom pods
75g unrefined golden caster sugar,
  plus extra for the topping

6 egg yolks
50g tinned Alphonso mango purée
  (alternatively blitz fresh mangoes
  in a food processor)
2 Alphonso mangoes, peeled and diced

1 Preheat the oven to 150°C/gas 2.

2 Pour the cream into a pan and then add the vanilla and cardamom pods. Bring the cream to a boil, then reduce the heat and simmer gently for 5 minutes.

3 Meanwhile, in a separate bowl, beat the sugar and egg yolks together in a large heatproof bowl until fluffy. Bring the cream back to boiling point and remove and discard the vanilla and cardamom pods. Pour the hot, aromatic cream over the egg mixture, whisking constantly until thickened. Strain the mixture through a fine sieve into a large jug, and then stir in the mango purée.

4 Put a layer of diced mango into the bottom of six ramekins, reserving a little for decoration, and then fill them to about two-thirds full with the cream mixture. Place the ramekins into a large roasting tray and fill with enough hot water to come halfway up their outsides. Place the roasting tray (which is now a bain-marie) very carefully on the middle shelf of the oven and cook for 40–45 minutes, or until the custards are just set but still a bit wobbly in the middle.

5 Remove the ramekins from the water and set aside to cool to room temperature. When you are ready to serve, sprinkle one level teaspoon of caster sugar evenly over the surface of each crème brûlée, then caramelise with a chef's blowtorch (alternatively place under a very hot grill for a few minutes until the sugar turns golden and starts to bubble). Top with the rest of the diced mango and serve.

BANANA LATTICE SERVES 6-8

This is a great way to use those bananas that are turning black in the fruit bowl. It's an easy dessert that uses ready-made pastry to turn ageing fruit into something quite delicious.

2 x 500-g packets shortcrust pastry
20g unsalted butter
5 large over-ripe bananas, chopped
60g unrefined golden caster sugar
25g desiccated coconut

25g ground almonds
1 vanilla pod, seeds scraped
  (see page 11)
1 tsp ground mixed spice
1 egg yolk, mixed with 1 tsp water

1 Preheat the oven to 180°C/gas 4.

2 Roll out one block of pastry and use to line a 23-cm loose-bottomed flan tin. Line the pastry with non-stick baking paper, weigh it down with baking beans and bake 'blind' for 15–20 minutes, or until the pastry is lightly golden. Baking blind will give you an even bake before adding the mixture and will help prevent a 'soggy bottom'.

3 Meanwhile, melt the butter in a large, heavy-based pan and allow to brown. Quickly add the bananas, sugar, coconut, almonds, vanilla seeds and mixed spice and cook, stirring, over a medium heat for about 5 minutes, until the mixture turns into a thick paste. Tip this mixture into the cooked pastry case and spread to the edges.

4 Roll out the second block of pastry and cut long strips about 0.5cm thick. Any unused pastry can be wrapped in cling film and placed in the fridge or freezer until you need to use it. Use the strips to form a lattice over the mixture, criss-crossing the strips as you lay them. Once the lattice is complete, brush the pastry with the egg yolk and water mixture and place directly into the oven. Cook for a further 30–40 minutes, until the lattice is golden brown.

TAPIOCA PUDDING SERVES 6

I remember growing up and my mum making the most delicious tapioca pudding at home and then having it at school and wondering what had happened to my favourite dessert! I think a lot of people have bad tapioca pudding memories, but I hope this recipe will reignite a relationship with this wonderful ingredient.

1 x 400ml tin coconut milk
100ml passion fruit juice
80g tapioca
100g unrefined golden caster sugar
3 cloves
4 cardamom pods, lightly crushed

1 star anise
4 fresh passion fruit, seeds and pulp
1 ripe papaya, peeled and
 cut into 2.5cm dice
1 ripe mango, peeled and
 cut into 2.5cm dice

1 Place the coconut milk and passion fruit juice in a pan and heat gently until the mixture starts to simmer – this should take about 4–5 minutes.

2 Strain the mixture through a fine sieve into a clean pan. Add the tapioca, sugar, cloves, cardamom and star anise and heat gently until the sugar has dissolved. Bring to a simmer and continue to cook, stirring occasionally, for 15 minutes, or until the tapioca balls have just turned translucent and the mixture has started to become sticky. Remove from the heat.

3 Fold in the fresh passion fruit seeds and pulp, along with the diced papaya and mango and serve immediately.

COCONUT SWEETS MAKES 20-25

I don't think I could have written this book and not have included
this recipe. It is so easy to prepare and is really fun to make with kids.
I remember my mum treating herself to a bar of this brilliant white
and pink sweet; it was her way of relaxing!

200ml water
275g unrefined golden caster sugar
1 vanilla pod, seeds scraped
   (see page 11)

2–3 brown coconuts, flesh grated
   (see Note)
few drops of pink food colouring
   (optional)

1 Start by making a simple sugar syrup. Place the water, sugar and food
colouring (if using) in a heavy-based pan and add the vanilla seeds. Heat
until the sugar has dissolved and the liquid has reduced by a quarter.

2 Add the grated coconut and stir through gently to allow the coconut to
soak up the syrup. Once this has happened, roll a teaspoon of the mixture
in your hands into a ball and place directly onto a lined baking tray. Leave
to cool – you can speed this up by placing it in the fridge if you can't wait!

NOTE
If you can't get hold of fresh coconuts, use 300g desiccated coconut instead
(although the flavour won't be as delicate).

MANGO, RUM AND LIME SYLLABUB

SERVES 4

4 ginger biscuits, crushed
300ml double cream
½ vanilla pod, seeds scraped (see page 11)
3 tbsp unrefined icing sugar
75ml rum, plus 4 tsp
zest and juice of 4 limes
150ml tinned Alphonso mango purée
   (alternatively blitz fresh mangoes
   in a food processor)

2 Alphonso mangoes, peeled
   and cut into 2.5cm cubes
desiccated coconut to sprinkle
   over the top
mint leaves, to decorate (optional)

1 Put the ginger biscuits into a large plastic bag (a sandwich bag is ideal) and bash vigorously with a rolling pin until you have a bag of crumbs.

2 Using an electric whisk, lightly whip the double cream. Add the vanilla seeds, icing sugar, the 75ml of rum, lime juice and zest, reserving a little for decoration. Keep whisking until it forms light peaks. Add about one-third of the mango purée and half the cubed mango and fold through for a marbled effect.

3 To assemble the syllabubs, divide the crumbs between 4 glasses. Sprinkle a teaspoon of rum over each and top with the rest of the mango purée. Spoon the cream over the top. Just before serving, sprinkle with desiccated coconut and reserved lime zest. Decorate with the mint leaves, if using.

GATEAU PATATE MAKES 8-10

I remember making these sweet potato and coconut cakes with Mum: I was so impatient that once the cakes were cooked I would grab the ones she had just fried and bite into them. The coconut syrup used to burn my mouth! Take my advice and let these cakes cool down slightly. They are delicious served warm with a lovely vanilla ice cream.

300g sweet potato, peeled
  and cut into chunks
pinch of salt
2 tbsp ground almonds
2–3 brown coconuts, flesh grated,
  or 100g desiccated coconut

100g unrefined golden caster sugar
1 tsp ground cinnamon
1 tsp good-quality vanilla extract
vegetable oil for deep-frying
vanilla ice cream, to serve

1 Cook the sweet potato in a large pan of boiling water with just a pinch of salt until tender, about 15–20 minutes. Drain and mash until completely smooth (use a potato ricer if you have one). Add the ground almonds and work into the mixture until you have a dough that comes together in a ball. Place in an oiled bowl, cover with a damp cloth and chill in the fridge for 30 minutes.

2 In a separate bowl, mix together the grated coconut, sugar, cinnamon and vanilla extract until well combined.

3 Once the dough has firmed up, divide the mixture into 8–10 small balls. Use a rolling pin to roll the balls into circles about 10cm in diameter. Place a teaspoon of the coconut mixture into the centre of each dough circle and then fold over to make a half-moon shape. Press down the edges using a fork so that none of the mixture can come out.

4 Heat enough vegetable oil for deep-frying in a large, heavy-based pan, until a cube of bread dropped in turns golden in 30 seconds. Alternatively heat a deep-fat fryer to 180°C. Fry the cakes for 4–5 minutes until golden brown and the pastry has puffed up. Drain on kitchen paper and leave to cool a little before serving. Serve warm with vanilla ice cream.

CHOCOLATE SAMOSAS MAKES 12

This is my take on a traditional savoury dish. Filling samosas with chocolate and coconut makes a really interesting dessert. Make these in advance and warm for a few minutes in the oven before serving.

200g white chocolate
75g desiccated coconut

1 packet samosa wrappers (look
    in Asian or Indian supermarkets)
melted butter

1 Preheat the oven to 200°C/gas 6.

2 Break the white chocolate into small pieces with your hands and place in a bowl. Mix in the desiccated coconut.

3 Take a samosa wrapper and place a tablespoon of the chocolate and coconut mixture at the top left corner of the rectangle. Fold the top right corner over the mixture to make a triangle. Fold this triangle over and keep going until you have a samosa. To bind the samosa together and to make sure the mixture doesn't come out, dab the corners with some water: this will act like a glue to stick the corners down.

4 Brush each samosa with melted butter on all sides and place on a baking tray lined with non-stick baking paper. Place directly into the oven and cook for about 8 minutes, or until the pastry is golden brown on the outside. Serve hot.

POUTOU
(STEAMED RICE CAKES)

MAKES 12

This is one of my mum's favourite cakes and reminds her of her childhood when she would buy these from street stalls after school and sometimes before. They are made using a very interesting technique; the dough is made in advance, snipped off and steamed in large steaming baskets. These ones are made with rice flour, although there are many variations across South East Asia. These are really easy to prepare and are quite unique in taste and texture.

300g rice flour
1 x 400ml tin coconut milk
80g unrefined golden caster sugar
1 egg, beaten
2 tbsp rosewater

few drops of pink food colouring/
  beetroot colouring (optional)
pinch of salt
1 tbsp baking powder

1 Bring a pan of water to the boil and place a bamboo steamer over it.

2 Mix all the ingredients together in a large mixing bowl until you have a thick batter. Place paper cupcake cases inside silicone cupcake moulds and fill until two-thirds full with the mixture – I like to use an ice cream scoop for this as I have found that it gives exactly the right amount of mixture for every cake.

3 Carefully place the cakes in the steaming basket and steam for 20 minutes, until firm to the touch. Serve warm.

ALMOND AND CINNAMON CAKE

SERVES 8-10

5 eggs, separated
1 tbsp good-quality vanilla extract
200g unrefined golden caster sugar
200g ground almonds
15g ground cinnamon
50g flaked almonds

TO DECORATE
unrefined icing sugar
cinnamon sticks

1 Preheat the oven to 180°C/gas 4 and grease and line a 23cm cake tin with non-stick baking paper.

2 Using an electric whisk, whisk the egg whites until stiff. In another bowl, whisk together the egg yolks, vanilla extract and sugar until completely pale and aerated.

3 Gently fold the ground almonds and ground cinnamon into the egg yolk mixture, being careful not to lose any air. Then fold in the beaten egg whites, again being careful not to overmix. Once the mixture is all combined, pour into the cake tin and sprinkle with the flaked almonds. Bake for around 40–50 minutes. To check whether the cake is cooked, insert a skewer; if it comes out clean the cake is done.

4 Allow the cake to cool in the tin. Remove from the tin and place on a plate or cake stand. Dust with icing sugar and decorate with pieces of broken cinnamon stick.

CHOCOLATE AND CARDAMOM COOKIES

MAKES 12–15 COOKIES

125g unsalted butter,
  at room temperature
100g unrefined golden caster sugar
70g unrefined dark muscovado sugar
1 egg, beaten
250g plain flour, sifted

pinch of salt
½ tsp baking powder
80g white chocolate, chopped
8 cardamom pods, crushed
  and black seeds removed

1 Preheat the oven to 180°C/gas 4.

2 Using an electric mixer cream together the butter and both sugars until light and fluffy. Mix in the egg, making sure it is completely incorporated. Add the sifted flour, salt and baking powder and mix until well combined. Fold in the white chocolate and cardamom seeds.

3 Line a baking tray or silicone baking mat with non-stick baking paper and use an ice-cream scoop to put dollops of mixture on to the tray. Make sure you leave plenty of space between them, so the cookies don't turn into twins!

4 Bake in the oven for 15 minutes. They may seem quite soft when they first come out but this is fine, as they will harden as they cool down. Cool completely on a wire rack before placing in a cookie jar – if they last that long!

NAPOLITAINES MAKES 12

This is such a classic Mauritian treat. You'll find this beautifully crisp shortbread filled with jam and covered with a bright pink glacé icing sold by vendors all over the island. I love these as they are so simple: definitely something to make when planning a tea party. They are also perfect to make with kids, as long as you don't mind getting messy.

300g plain flour, sifted
200g unsalted butter, at room temperature
250g unrefined icing sugar

few drops of pink food colouring (or colour of your choice)
75g good-quality strawberry jam

1 Preheat the oven to 160°C/gas 2½.

2 Place the flour in a large mixing bowl and cut the butter into small dice. Add to the flour and use the tips of your fingers to rub the flour and butter together until you form fine breadcrumbs. If the mixture seems too dry just add some more butter – don't be tempted to add water as you want the shortbread to be really crumbly and buttery. Bring the mixture together with your hands but do not knead the dough. Set aside for about 10 minutes.

3 Place a large sheet of non-stick baking paper on your work surface and place the dough in the middle. Cover with another piece of baking paper – this is so you can roll the dough without adding any more flour to the mixture. Roll the mixture to approximately 1.5cm thick and then cut shapes with a round 6cm cookie cutter. Place the shortbread on a baking tray lined with baking paper and bake in the oven for around 15–18 minutes until golden. Remove from the oven and allow to cool completely before moving them.

4 Mix the icing sugar with a few drops of food colouring and enough water to make a spreadable icing. Spread strawberry jam on to half the biscuits and sandwich with the remaining biscuits. Spread the top and sides of each biscuit with the coloured icing. Leave to dry for 1–2 hours before serving.

INDIAN SWEETMEAT

MAKES 20

This recipe is very similar to the Indian sweetmeat *barfi*, which has a fudge-like texture and is very sweet. It's usually reserved for big celebrations but I think it would make a lovely gift, especially to give to friends as part of a home-made hamper.

500g powdered milk
230ml milk
200g ground almonds
200g sugar

1 tbsp ground mixed spice
pinch of salt
70g pistachios, coarsely chopped

1 Place all the ingredients except the pistachios in a large heavy-based pan and cook over a medium heat for about 5–10 minutes, stirring continuously, until the mixture thickens and starts to stick to the pan. At this point remove from the heat and tip the mixture into a lightly oiled tray. Scatter the top with the chopped pistachios.

2 Allow the mixture to cool down before placing into the fridge. Chill for 2 hours. Once the fudge has set, cut into cubes. Store in an airtight container for up to 3 days or wrap in cellophane gift bags to give to friends.

COOL-DOWN DRINKS
AND COCKTAILS

No Mauritian meal is complete without an accompanying drink or cocktail. As a sugar-producing country, Mauritius is renowned for its beautiful rum, ranging from dark and sweet to smoky and almost whisky-like. Mauritian spiced rum can be hard to find in the UK so I've used other spirits as well, to create a range of 'sunshine' cocktails that will perk up the coldest of evenings. There are plenty of non-alcoholic drinks too, so there is something to suit the whole family.

ALOODA SERVES 8

This was a Persian drink that was brought over to South East Asia. It is called *faluda* in other countries, but in Mauritius it is known as *alooda*. This drink can be found on many street stalls in Port Louis, the capital of Mauritius, which actually sits on the tropic of cancer and is one of the most humid places on the island. *Alooda* is most definitely an acquired taste, but when you drink it in the city, it offers the most cooling effect in this subtropical climate. Bizarrely, it reminds me of the strawberry milkshake we used to make as kids using strawberry cordial. It has basil seeds and jelly in this mixture, but if you find the taste too strange you can most definitely leave them out – it will be just as refreshing.

400ml coconut milk (from a carton not a tin – I use Kara Coconut Milk)
600ml water
150g unrefined golden caster sugar
50g edible basil seeds (see Note)

1 tbsp good-quality vanilla extract
1 tbsp rosewater
2 leaves gelatine, soaked in cold water to soften
crushed ice, to serve

1 Put the coconut milk, water and sugar in a large serving jug and stir until the sugar has dissolved. Add the basil seeds, vanilla extract and rosewater, stir and leave to steep in the fridge for about 4 hours.

2 Place 220ml water in a pan and bring to a gentle simmer, then remove from the heat. Squeeze the excess water from the gelatine leaves and place them in the pan of hot water. Mix thoroughly until the gelatine has completely dissolved. Pour the mixture straight into a shallow container and leave to cool at room temperature before placing in the fridge to set.

3 To serve, chop the jelly into 2cm cubes and add to the coconut mixture in the jug, along with a cup of crushed ice. Give the mixture a really good stir and serve immediately. (Pictured on page 215, top right.)

NOTE

Edible basil seeds, also known as *tukmaria*, are the seeds from the Thai basil plant, not the more commonly seen Italian basil. You can buy the seeds at good Asian supermarkets. They can be left out or replaced with poppy seeds if necessary.

MANGO MOJITO WITH SPICED COLD RUM SERVES 1

handful mint leaves, roughly torn
1 tbsp unrefined golden caster sugar
juice of 1 lime
2 tbsp mango purée (you can
  buy tinned or make your own
  by blending fresh mango)

½ tsp freshly grated ginger
25ml spiced rum
½ cup crushed ice
75ml soda water
lime wedge and cubes of mango,
  to serve

1 Place the mint leaves, sugar and lime juice in the bottom of a tall glass and use the end of a rolling pin to 'muddle' them i.e. bash them together. Add the mango purée, ginger and rum and stir thoroughly. Add the crushed ice and top with the soda water.

2 Serve with a wedge of lime along with some fresh pieces of mango. (Pictured on page 217, far right.)

MAURITIAN RUM CAIPIRINHA SERVES 1

2 limes
1 tsp light muscovado sugar
25ml spiced Mauritian rum

25ml cachaça
ice cubes

1 Cut each lime into quarters and place in a large jug.

2 Using a large pestle or the end of a rolling pin, bash the fruit, then add the sugar, rum and cachaça and mix together until well combined.

3 Strain over ice and serve immediately. (Pictured on page 217, bottom left.)

BELLE MARE SERVES 1

This recipe is dedicated to my mum – Belle Mare is her favourite beach in Mauritius. This cocktail is sweet and fruity with a lovely tart flavour.

1 tbsp palm sugar
juice of 2 limes
50ml spiced Mauritian rum
50ml Blue Curaçao

100ml soda water
50ml fresh passion fruit juice
  (see Note)
lime wedge, to garnish

1 In a large jug, mix together the palm sugar and lime juice until the sugar has dissolved. Add the rum and Blue Curaçao and stir well, finally adding the soda water.

2 Half-fill a glass with ice and then pour over the rum mixture. Pour the passion fruit juice over the top and garnish with a wedge of lime.

NOTE
Strain the pulp from approximately 6 passion fruit to get 50ml of fresh juice – different fruit yield different amounts of juice.

RUM, ELDERFLOWER AND COCONUT COCKTAIL SERVES 1

20ml elderflower cordial
50ml spiced dark rum
100ml coconut milk

ice cubes
desiccated coconut

1 Place all the ingredients except the desiccated coconut into a cocktail shaker and shake vigorously until well combined. Pour over ice and sprinkle with the coconut. (Pictured on page 217, top left.)

LYCHEE BOBA TEA SERVES 6-8

I made this on *MasterChef* for the Prince of Thailand and it was one of the dishes that he found very amusing. I wasn't sure whether that was a good or bad thing, but in retrospect, I think anything that makes people laugh or smile can't be a bad thing. This drink is very popular across South East Asia and comes in many guises; this is my take.

50g large dried black tapioca pearls
  (see Note)
½ x 425g tin lychees in syrup
2 tbsp jasmine tea leaves

400ml coconut milk
150ml evaporated milk
ice cubes, to serve

1 Place the tapioca pearls in a pan with 600ml of water and cook over a medium heat until the pearls turn black and jelly-like. Drain and set aside.

2 Using a stick blender or a food processor, blitz the lychees, including their syrup, until completely smooth.

3 Put the tea leaves, coconut milk and evaporated milk into a separate heavy-based pan, and allow to come to a gentle simmer. Strain the mixture and allow to cool before adding the lychee purée, then place in the fridge to chill for 2 hours.

4 Once cold, place in a large jug, add the tapioca pearls and a handful of ice cubes and serve. (Pictured opposite, left.)

NOTE
Black tapioca pearls can be bought online or at specialist Asian supermarkets. You could substitute with white tapioca pearls, although the contrast in colour and flavour are not quite the same.

SWEET AND SOUR REFRESHER SERVES 4

70g tamarind pulp
50g unrefined light muscovado sugar
pinch of salt

700ml boiled water
crushed ice, to serve
juice of 1 lime, to serve

1 Put the tamarind pulp, sugar, salt and boiled water in a blender and blitz until smooth.

2 Strain this mixture into a mixing jug and leave to cool before placing in the fridge to chill for 2 hours.

3 Just before serving add ice and freshly squeezed lime juice.

PINA COLADA MOCKTAIL SERVES 4

3 over-ripe bananas
500ml pineapple juice
100ml coconut milk

150g ice cubes
fresh pineapple, to garnish

1 Place everything in a blender and blitz until completely smooth.

2 Serve in hi-ball tumblers and garnish with fresh pineapple.

MANGO FEVER SERVES 2

100ml Alphonso mango purée
  (you can buy tinned or make
  your own by blending fresh
  mango)
juice of 2 limes
100ml sanguinello blood orange juice

100ml pineapple juice
6–8 ice cubes

TO GARNISH
sprig of mint
lime wedges

1 Place all the ingredients in a blender and blitz until completely combined.

2 Serve in tumblers or martini glasses with fresh lime and mint. (Pictured on page 215, right.)

SWEET AND SPICY TEA OVER ICE SERVES 4–6

2 tbsp masala chai tea
1 tsp ground cinnamon
1 tsp mixed spiced
1 x 400ml tin coconut milk

200ml water
3 tbsp unrefined light muscovado sugar
1 tsp good-quality vanilla extract
ice cubes, to serve

1 Put all the ingredients, except the ice, into a large pan and heat until the liquid comes to a simmer and the tea has infused into the mixture.

2 Strain the liquid into a tall serving jug and allow to cool before placing in the fridge to chill completely, about 2 hours.

3 Add ice to individual glasses and pour the tea over the ice.

INDEX

ACKNOWLEDGEMENTS

This book could never have been written without the support and encouragement of my family and friends over all these years. Without you I'm nothing, and with you I've become who I am. I could dedicate a whole page to everyone who has touched my life, but then there wouldn't be any space left for recipes!

Firstly, to my Mum, the biggest influence in my life, who encouraged me to be the person I am. She has taught me so much and let me become the woman I am today.

The other significant Permalloos: Kevin, Pam, Jim and the boys, for being my constant rock throughout all the hard times and for being there to smile and laugh with.

To Mr. Vinci, for putting up with me and supporting me all the way, for opening my eyes to new cuisines and for being my guinea pig. And to the Vinci family for opening their Italian kitchen to me and allowing me to be experience their wonderful culture and cuisine, especially Papa Alberto for the hours of eating and talking about food.

Uncle and Aunty for always being the best, and for continuing to love me! Vik and Brinda for being the best cousins.

Athar, for his love of potato salad and for always bashing away my demons.

Russell, for introducing me to saltfish and ackee, a moment in time none of us could ever forget!

The Brunel girls, who provided me with hours of laughter, gossip and a bit of studying. We have shared some great food moments: the corned beef stew, Serwah's incredible cajun chicken and, of course, the bitten cheese in the fridge – you know who you are!

Gurp, for being my maid of honour and for being a bad boy food tester! Bola and Kontoh, my sisters from another mother, which time apart cannot change.

Yvonne and Tolu for the jokes throughout the years. I couldn't even begin to write down all the support you've given me. Inspired.

Poonam, for her love of everything sweet and mutual appreciation of Encona hot sauce.

Lee, Keri and Anna, for recognising my talent from a young age and for being the girls that I go to for everything. The tears and (roars of) laughter have helped me become the woman I am and the woman I will be.

Luca, for his love of coconut and spices. Alice & Harry for finding friendship in a time when we were all going through change – thank you for being there for me.

Jonny McWilliams, my agent, who has now become a real friend and someone I can turn to and always trust. Thank you for making this dream come true.

Jonathan Conway, from recognising my book writing talents right at the beginning and supporting me so early on in my career.

To my editor, Sarah Lavelle, for encouraging me throughout this process and giving all her support.

To the best photographer in town, Martin Poole. Thank you for Mauritius and for making my food look the best it ever could.

The team at Smith & Gilmour, for coming to Mauritius and creating one of the most beautiful recipe books I could have imagined.

Aya and Richard Harris for their beautiful food styling and help with the recipes. Thank you also to Lydia, for creating the perfect props for the book and going above and beyond to make the book so special.

Clare Sayer, for the hours of book editing and masses of emails back and forth!

Lou and Bev and the team at Plank PR for their ongoing support.

To Holly and Rox and all the Team at Wasserman.

A special thank you to Ray and Leynah, and the team at Billingtons, for introducing me to the full range of beautiful Mauritian sugars. Thanks also to Simply Be, Maradiva Villas Resort and Spa, KitchenAid and Cuisinart.

To the MC Crew – Karen Ross, Clare Nosworthy, the two Daves, John Gilbert, Vicky Howarth, Lisa, Dhruv, Katie Atwood and Elizabeth Fisher, for being there right at the beginning and helping me to push through into my new career, and for the many hours of looking after me on the show!

John and Gregg for recognising my true gift and for continuing to support and advise me as I go on this journey – in particular helping me to stay true to myself and rid me of my self doubt!

The SW crew for drinking with me, in particular the Clarence lot. Tom, Koj and Jay for sharing this moment with me, as well as Thailand, drinks, drinks, tears and more drinks! Without you guys I don't know what would have happened.

Manake and Naky, for introducing me to the best brie I've ever had and their EPIC house parties. Cita, for always being there to crack open that bottle and babble away with for hours.

To my friends in Southampton who I grew up with.

To my family and fellow islanders in Mauritius.

To all the incredible chefs I've had the honour of cooking for and with during and after MasterChef.